SEO Like I'm 5

The Ultimate Beginner's Guide to Search Engine Optimization

by Matthew Capala

Editorial direction by Steven C. Baldwin

Cover design by Natalie Leeke

Published by Kindle Self Publishing LLC

New York, 2014

ISBN-13: 978-1500865207

ISBN-10: 1500865206

Praise for 'SEO Like I'm 5'

'SEO Like I'm 5' is written in a way that is accessible to anyone who is curious about how SEO really works without spending a lot of time on theory. The book is perfect for beginners who are interested in quickly learning best practices and want to understand what they need to do next to get the most out of their website.

Linda Gharib, SVP, Digital Marketing at Citigroup, Adj. Professor at Baruch College, Internet Marketing

I've known Matt Capala for years... If you ever have an opportunity to meet him in a professional capacity, you'll find that Matt has a way of energizing people to believe they can succeed at otherwise complicated marketing activities.

With 'SEO Like I'm 5' he's distilled the whirlwind of insights that float around the Web unfettered and made them actionable for everyone. Chock full of tools, best practices and action items that help get the reader started, Matt's done a great job of taking everything he's learned throughout his career and giving it to the reader in an easy-to-digest capsule. While SEO has gotten harder than ever, Matt explains it in a way that will help you get in the game with a winning playbook.

Michael King, Featured Author of 'Inbound Marketing and SEO: Insights from the Moz Blog,' Founder, iPullRank and Quantum Lead

A refreshing look at SEO... In his recent book, 'SEO Like I'm 5,' Matthew Capala emphasizes the need to learn and practice SEO...like it's 2014. He explains effective SEO strategies in a way that doesn't require the advanced technical knowledge that can become a barrier for those that generally need it the most.

Jonathan Cho, Managing Director, Head of Search and Social at Mindshare

Having been in the industry for many years and having read many books on marketing and SEO, I was skeptical to read yet another book that claims it will change my business for the better. Matthew Capala's 'SEO Like I'm 5' is practical, actionable, and clear. The book does two things well. It's instructive in case I decide to do SEO myself, but perhaps its even bigger value is if I decide to hire someone else to do it for me. I highly recommend this book to any solopreneur.

Dino Dogan, Founder and CEO of Triberr, Co-Author (w/ Guy Kawasaki and Mark Schaefer) of 'Engagement from Scratch: How Super-Community Builders Create a Loyal Audience and How You Can Do the Same!'

I've had a chance to interview a number of SEO spammers in my career as a journalist. Sadly, they all share an obsession with fast money, contempt for the searchers tricked into consuming their low-quality content, and the strangely irrational belief that they'll always be able to operate outside the reach of the law.

Today, however, as Matt Capala points out in 'SEO Like I'm 5,' the "Wild West Era of SEO" is over, a new sheriff is in town, and civilization is about to arrive on the search frontier. The good news is that marketers using Matt's approach will actually profit much more over time than those using the crude, risky optimization tactics of the past.

Stephen C. Baldwin
Author of 'Net Slaves: True Tales of Working the Web,' (McGraw-Hill), Editor-in-Chief at Didit

Matt Capala wrote 'SEO Like I'm 5' for people – regular people like you and me – not doctoral research fellows studying Semiotics, Semantics, or Information Theory. While it addresses the important mechanics of how search engines work, how they understand Web content, and the optimization tasks required for better visibility, its main focus is empowering you, using an accessible workshop style, with the SEO tools you'll need to build real influence on the Internet.

Kevin Lee
CEO and Exec. Chairman at Didit, Author of 'The Eyes Have It: How to Market in an Age of Divergent Consumers, Media Chaos, and Advertising Anarchy,' Founding Board Member of SEMPO

Having known Matthew Capala for a number of years, he has taught me a great deal about SEO. In his new book, 'SEO Like I'm 5' he imparts this depth and understanding in a simplified and straight-forward way that one can understand just by reading the material on how to improve their SEO...and therefore, their revenue and profits.

Kathleen Murray, Angel Investor, Chair of Executive Forum Angels, President of Harvard Business School Women's Association

Contents

About the Author

Matthew Capala is a growth-focused Internet marketer and entrepreneur. With over a decade of digital marketing experience working with some of the world's largest brands (Apple, Western Union, Smirnoff, Dell, LG, Prudential), successful entrepreneurs and emerging startups, Matthew has leveraged the Internet in unprecedented ways to spur growth.

He is the founder of SearchDecoder.com, Adj. Professor at NYU, consultant, dynamic speaker, trainer, blogger and author. Formerly, Head of Search and Content Marketing at Lowe Profero (the Americas), where he built a million dollar business ground-up, growing the group from two to nine employees in under two years. In 2014, Matthew built a nimble growth marketing company, CENSEO, to service funded startups, and Fortune 500 brands that want to innovate and grow like startups.

Matthew has spoken at various industry conferences and trained workshops all over the world, including New York, Miami, San Francisco London, Vienna, Munich, and Warsaw. He writes for several industry leading blogs and publications, including The Next Web, Sparksheet, Medium, and Problogger.

Matthew Capala grew up in Poland and emigrated to New York a decade ago, where he has led several lives: construction worker, scaffold operator, waiter, Internet marketer, executive, professor, and entrepreneur. In that order.

Internet entrepreneurship and SEO enabled me to create opportunities in life I wouldn't have had otherwise

- Matthew Capala

He is the author of a widely-praised free personal branding e-book, 'Away with the Average,' in which he shares his hard-won advice on how to leverage the Internet and social media to get ahead of the pack. You can find it at AwayWithAverage.com.

Matthew has a BA in International Relations and an MA in American Studies from the University of Lodz. He holds a Marketing MBA from Baruch College (class of 2008).

You can contact him on Twitter at @SearchDecoder.

Foreword

by Kevin Lee

I've been working in Search Marketing for almost 20 years now (my firm, Didit.com, launched in 1996). When I look back over the many developments that have affected the search ecosystem over the years, there's never been more of a need for clear, accurate, actionable information about SEO. Why?

Because in search, things change all the time. Search engines used to employ very simple formulas to determine the merit of a given Web page or site. Today they use hundreds of factors, and their algorithms are continually being tweaked – even on a daily basis.

Because when things change, they become complex. Once upon a time, marketers could perform a few optimization actions, relax, and see the traffic (and orders) roll in. Today, marketers need to master multiple online marketing methods, deploy them instantly, and continually revise them to stay competitive.

Because when things become complex, confusion is in far greater supply than clarity. Search engines are much less willing to disclose the details of their operations than they were several years ago. A lot of information that was once provided freely to 3rd parties is drying up. Details about major algorithmic updates (for example Google's Hummingbird) aren't published at all. When the supply of objective data is scarce, conjecture (and sometimes paranoia) quickly fills the knowledge vacuum, fueled by consultants seeking to profit from this confusion. What's missing is clarity – and a clear way forward.

Which brings me to 'SEO Like I'm 5.' Matt Capala wrote this book for people – regular people like you and me – not doctoral research fellows studying Semiotics, Semantics, or Information Theory. While it addresses the important mechanics of how search engines work, how they understand Web content, and the optimization tasks required for better visibility, its main focus is empowering you – using an accessible workshop style – with the tools you'll need to build real influence on the Internet.

'SEO Like I'm 5 is also timely. It takes account of Google's latest algorithm updates, including Penguin, Panda, and Hummingbird (if you've never heard of these weirdly-named algorithms, Matt will set you straight) and tells you how they should influence your Web content strategy. And while the book quite properly focuses on the nuts and bolts of SEO you'll need to get ahead, it doesn't treat this discipline in isolation. Matt reaches out to experts from SEO, social media, blogging, PR, and monetization communities to understand SEO in its proper context.

Finally – and it's one of my favorite things about 'SEO Like I'm 5' – Matt accomplishes something that is very difficult for any writer to do: to take a complex, jargon-laden subject and communicate its essence in a way that any thinking person will understand and act upon. Because SEO – like any marketing methodology – is really just a means to an end, the end being the achievement of your business, personal, and professional goals.

If you follow the teachings in this book, I have no doubt that your path to these goals will be measurably advanced.

Kevin Lee
Author of 'The Eyes Have It: How to Market in an Age of Divergent Consumers, Media Chaos, and Advertising Anarchy,' CEO at Didit, Advisory Board at eMarketing Association, Founding Board Member of SEMPO

Introduction

Make no mistake; this is **no** 'SEO for dummies.'

Rather, 'SEO Like I'm 5' is the ultimate beginner's training system for forward-thinking businesses and entrepreneurs that will get you found on Google, social media, and blogs.

You will also learn how to attract followers and leads like a magnet by building a vibrant community around your content, which both users and search engines will love, and leveraging untapped, high-growth platforms and social networks.

In addition to taking you through the strategic process of building and optimizing your online presence, 'SEO Like I'm 5' features hundreds of free tools, 'under-the-hood' hacks, case studies, examples, and actionable tips.

Why Read this Book?

There is an overload of information on the topic of SEO on the Web, most of it misguided or outdated, coming from self-proclaimed gurus.

Contrary to common knowledge, the 'art of SEO' is not defined by your ability to write code or hack Google's algorithm. The truth is that today, online success has more to do with your ability to create amazing content, establish a strong social media presence, and build relationships with bloggers than writing lines of code or stuffing keywords into your meta data.

'SEO Like I'm 5' takes you through an action-oriented, workshop-style, pain-free process to plan, build, and optimize your online presence, including:

— Where to start
— Which free platforms and tools to use
— How to build a search-friendly website
— How to build a killer content strategy
— How to become a rockstar blogger
— How to find the golden-nugget keyword opportunities
— How to monetize your website
— How to attract backlinks to your content
— How to build relationships with bloggers and influencers

— How to build a winning social media strategy

— How to make money online

Who is this Book for?

— Entrepreneurs and startups

— Forward-thinking small business owners

— Marketing executives who want to learn how to innovate like startups

— Students and professionals

— Authors, artists, and bloggers

The cool thing about 'SEO Like I'm 5' is that it offers more than just text. It comes with hundreds of screenshots and step-by-step instructions you can actually use while reading it.

Moreover, you will find the book at times quite entertaining, which makes a dry topic of SEO fun for those who are just starting out.

SEO = Growth

SEO is rooted in the philosophy of growth.

The foundation of growth, and thus SEO, lies in your ability to design and follow a process where every small step *compounds* into big results. The secret is in your ability to see ahead and stay consistent, which is easier said than done.

Kevin Lee, the CEO of Didit, calls this phenomenon *compound marketing*.

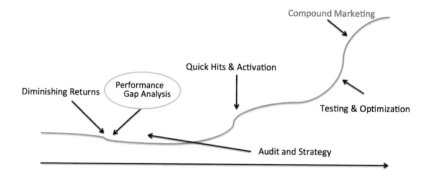

Online growth and SEO are predicated on holistic thinking. In

addition to the *usual suspects,* such as keyword research, link building, and meta tag optimization, 'SEO Like I'm 5' introduces a holistic approach to the process of gaining online visibility.

It emphasises the signals and metrics that *post-Hummingbird* Google cares about today, including the knowledge graph, Google+, social content, community engagement, user experience, and semantics.

Teamwork Makes the Dream Work

'SEO Like I'm 5' was a collaborative effort. It includes two years of meticulous research in the field and classrooms of NYU, as well as hundreds of interviews with the top SEOs in the world.

Imagine a curated team of world-class, hand-picked SEO mentors, coaches, practitioners, trainers, bloggers and professors coming together to impart their hard-won knowledge and share tried-and-proven, under-the-hood tips and tools to help you grow your website, business, or hobby online.

Here you will not find any self-proclaimed SEO gurus who spend all day on the SEO forums and blogs arguing about what Matt Cutts (head of Google's webspam team) said or meant to say. This book is not about debating or speculation; it's about actionable strategies from in-the-trenches Internet veterans to help you succeed.

The experts and collaborators featured in this book represent various areas of SEO and bring their specialized knowledge to bear on a variety of topics, including content marketing, analytics, social media, digital PR, online monetization, and link building.

Acknowledgements

Special thanks to Amrita Saha, my former NYU student, who has been part of this project since its inception through research, contribution, editing and marketing; Steve Baldwin, who offered me amazing editorial feedback; and Joseph McKeating, who helped me edit the book working out of Hawaii!

Here is the list of contributors who worked with me in various capacities to make this book a success. In no particular order.

Stephen C. Baldwin, Author of 'Net Slaves: True Tales of Working the Web' (McGraw-Hill)

Amrita Saha, Recent NYU grad and digital marketing professional

Joseph McKeating, Founder of Pulsar Strategy

Ana Raynes, Director of Social Media at Didit

Brian Dean, Founder of Backlinko

Brian Honigman, Writer for Mashable, Huffington Post, Entrepreneur, and Forbes

Clayburn Griffin, Founder of /r/BigSEO on Reddit, Content Strategist at i360

Paul Shapiro, SEO Director at Catalyst (a WPP company)

Jenny Halasz, President at JLH Marketing, Columnist for Search Engine Land

Andrew Wong, Founder and CEO of Coinvent

Mike Fishbein, Founder of Startup College

Mike King, Founder of iPullRank, Global Moz Associate

Brooke Ballard, Founder of B Squared Media

Lisha Klopper, Manager at Gyro

Jason White, SEO Director at Dragon Search

Brady D. Callahan, Lead SEO Strategist at UpTik Media

Ryan Bidduplh, Founder of BloggingFromParadise.com

Kristi Hines, Pro-Blogger, Writer for Search Engine Watch

Newsdesk Team at Didit.com

Inbound Marketing Clinic at NYU SCPS

Like all the best contemporary books on the topic of Internet marketing, 'SEO Like I'm 5' was born on blogs, forums, and social media. Some of the early chapters and interviews were featured on my blogs. Big thanks to all the readers who offered me tons of great feedback over the last couple of months.

How to Get the Best Value Reading the Book

Do things, tell people.

You would not believe how much opportunity is out there for those who do things and tell people. You build something online that is interesting and you tell everyone about it, online and offline.

Then you get traffic that leads to contracts or job offers. You make a lot of friends who think what you do is cool.

Then, the next time someone needs to solve a problem related to that cool thing, they come to you first. You become an expert and Google will get you on the front page of it's search results on the keywords that describe the things that you **do** and talk about, not the other way around.

Use this book for building things online to get optimal results, and share your progress with the community on Twitter using hashtag #SEOLike5 to get support and feedback.

Marketing Like It's 2014

'80% of success is showing up', Woody Allen famously said about life.

Marketing in 2014 is not much different. You need to show up when consumers search for your product or service on Google, when you are spoken about on social media, or when you receive a review or a comment.

Why? Because **showing up equals cash**:

80% of consumers search for a product/service before purchasing it

70% read online reviews before making purchase decisions

68% of consumers begin their decision-making while searching for a keyword

Websites that blog regularly receive **55%** more traffic and over 80% more leads compared to websites that don't

Over **70%** of search clicks are organic

The list goes on. But you don't need a litany of statistics to know that showing up on the Internet reaps big profits. You already know it. We all turn to Google, social media, review blogs, and other places on the Web when we make most decisions in life in 2014, including purchase decisions. It's a fact.

Yet, many businesses still miss out on the vast opportunities search engines, blogs, and social media have to offer. They fail to show up when consumers search for or talk about them. At the focal point of decision making, when the purchase intent is as high as it gets, they leave money on the table.

Do You Show Up?

Do a quick test, right now and right here on your mobile phone. Google a couple of keywords that best describe your product or service. Not your brand keywords, but more generic terms.

Whether we are shopping for a digital camera, plane tickets, or a honeymoon in Costa Rica, the Internet has changed how we decide what to buy. John Lesicki of Google describes this new decision-making process as the 'Zero Moment of Truth.'

You can find his free ebook under the same title at ZeroMomementOfTruth.com. It's required reading in the graduate search marketing class I teach at NYU.

Showing Up is 80% of Success

Today, you are not only behind technology, you are behind the consumer.

If they can't find you, you don't exist. If you don't talk to them, you are not relevant. Without awesome content, you are boring.

In a world where 80% of consumers search for a product or service before purchasing it...

Invisibility is a fate much worse than failure. Tweet this if you agree with a hashtag #SEOLike5.

Search engines, blogs, and social media are not the future of business; the shift already happened. Have you missed the boat? It's time to get your act together and figure out that damned Google algorithm!

Are your sales falling despite skyrocketing investments in ads? It's because only around 0.10% of people click on banner ads today. So the ad industry counts and charges for 'impressions,' a third of which are not even seen by humans. 86% skip TV ads. 44% of direct mail never gets opened. The list goes on.

There is just too much going over the Internet for consumers to ever enjoy being interrupted.

Marketing in 2014 and beyond is not about interrupting consumers when they enjoy content. It is about 'being' that content.

Excuses for Not Marketing Like It's 2014

There are many reasons why you may not be using inbound marketing channels (such as SEO, blogging, social media, and newsletters) to drive leads.

You might have tried, got burned, and given up. I hear it all the time. Trust me, it's not that inbound marketing is not working for you, it's the other way around; you haven't made it work for you.

You might have even gotten in trouble with Google or Facebook for being irresponsible. Examples include outsourcing your social media to an intern or hiring an SEO company in India that guaranteed to 'get you on top of Google for 10 keywords' for a couple hundred bucks.

Be human. Both users and algorithms will smell a phony. Tweet this if you agree with a hashtag #SEOLike5.

The landscape has changed a lot. Old tactics have been rendered obsolete. You can no longer outsource tweeting, link building, or blogging. You can certainly hire a consultant or an agency to help you, but they cannot 'be' you. Your content needs to be native, authentic, and human. You need to be involved.

The Time is NOW

The good news is that the time has never been better for small businesses and bootstrap marketers to reach mass audiences.

New digital tools have emerged to make it possible for individuals and businesses to make millions of dollars online without any significant cost to start a business and promote it. The barriers to entry do not exist anymore. Smart marketers can now reach mass media audiences without spending millions of dollars, simply by ranking first on Google or YouTube, or being influential on social networks.

And yet 80% of websites are marketing like it's early 2000. You can do better!

The New Lay of the Land

Recall the good old days of Google? White background and ten blue links.

At its inception, Google resembled a library-style catalogue for indexing and retrieving relevant information. The big idea at the time was to return the most relevant results based on relevancy (mentions of keywords) and authority factors (backlinks).

Google's ranking system was revolutionary at the time, but quickly became susceptible to spam. All it took to rank highly on Google results pages was to stuff your website with relevant keywords and buy links pointing to it.

Those days are over. Google now uses hundreds of various signals and thousands of bits of data to rank sites and pages.

While Google's algorithm evolved significantly over the last couple of years, the approach to SEO for many businesses has not caught up with the new reality. Consequently, their rankings dropped overnight.

Google's Time Machine

To visualize, let's time travel back to 2001 and search for one of the Google founders, Larry Page.

The top three search results at the time...

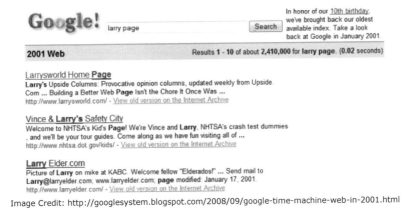

Image Credit: http://googlesystem.blogspot.com/2008/09/google-time-machine-web-in-2001.html

Now, **fast-forward to 2014:**

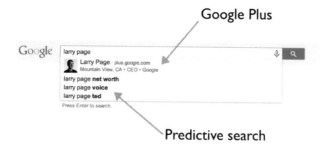

Google Plus

Predictive search

Google now provides new search features as early as when you start typing your keyword.

Predictive search recommends highly-searched, relevant queries matching your intent as you type. This Amazon-style recommendation engine is a great tool for keyword research. You want to study the targeted query recommendations from Google for the keywords you decide to target for your SEO campaign.

Did you also notice the Google+ listing at the top of the predictive stream of recommendations in the Google's search box?

Like it or not, Google Plus is — and will continue to be — one of the key building blocks of your SEO strategy.

Here is Google's SERP (Search Engine Result Page) for the same keyword in 2014.

The big change is that in 2014 **only about 15% of Google's SERP is made up of the blue links to relevant websites**.

Today, 85% of search engine results represent rich media (videos, images, graphics), information from the knowledge graph (more on this later), maps, local listings, social media, news, wikis, reviews, and many more new sources that Google is introducing every day.

Over time, Google has evolved from a matchmaker to a provider of information.

It's a big shift. Picture this: in the past, when you searched for 'weather in nyc,' Google would return results with 10 blue links to websites, such as accuweather.com or weather.com, that would generate a lot of traffic which in turn could be converted into dollars when ads were served against this traffic.

How much traffic do you think those weather sites are getting today from Google organic search?

Are you still interested in scrolling down to view and click on the old-time blue links under the 'boxed answer' Google now provides to users?

At the time of writing this chapter, I searched for movie showtimes at the Angelika Film Center. Check out Google's SERP below.

The area that this screenshot captured is called **above the fold**.

In other words, the part of the screen searchers see without scrolling down (where exactly 'the fold' is depends on the size and resolution of your screen).

Note Google's 'carousel' on the top, the real-time feed of showtimes on the left, and the Google map display pointing to the address of the theater location that's connected to Google+ Local. Good old blue links are becoming as dead as a dodo across an increasing number of keyword categories such as local.

Today, the first page of Google strives more and more to provide answers, not blue links to answers. Your SEO strategy must reflect this new reality.

The Search Engine Landscape

According to the most recent comScore report, 19.4 billion explicit core searches were conducted in March 2014, with Google Sites ranking first with 13.1 billion. Microsoft Sites ranked second with 3.6 billion searches, followed by Yahoo Sites with 2 billion, the Ask Network with 478 million, and AOL, Inc. with 259 million.

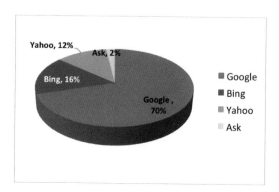

Google is leading the search engine market with a 70% share in the US. Yahoo is using Bing's search technology, and their combined market share in the U.S. is close to 30%. Ask.com and AOL license Google's search technology.

Globally, Google owns about 90% of the search market share.

Mobile search

Mobile search has redefined user and SERP experience.

Why should you be paying attention to mobile trends?

The use of mobile search has grown by **500%** over the past two years (Econsultancy).

82% of mobile shoppers use search to influence their purchasing decisions (Google Online Shopper Study).

Across all industries, mobile traffic is increasing by **3.5%** per month (Televox).

Of the estimated **30 billion** annual mobile searches, about 12 billion are local searches (Search Engine Land).

The explosion of mobile and local search has big SEO consequences. Most importantly, it means that you must make sure that the design of your website is **responsive** (which means that it works equally well on all devices, including traditional desktop/laptops, tablets, and smart phones). 44% of users will click to another mobile result if a site is not mobile-friendly (Icebreaker Consulting).

For the most part, many elements of desktop/laptop and mobile (smartphones and tablets) search are very similar. I recommend building your website and blog on Wordpress, which is responsive, so you don't need to worry about any mobile-specific SEO tactics at the outset.

The Evolution of SEO Ranking Factors

The ranking factors used by search engines to evaluate the objective merit of Web content have evolved dramatically over the last couple of years. New or updated algorithms have been rolled out taking aim at poor content (Panda), illicit link-building schemes (Penguin), and rewarding webmasters whose content has better credibility (Hummingbird).

Some signals Google formerly used to rely on for ranking intelligence have been completely discarded, including keyword meta data, due to their being systematically abused by black hat SEO spammers.

As a general rule of thumb, Google is moving away from any type of signals that can be manipulated manually (directory submissions, meta data, and commenting) in favor of signals that need to be earned, are natural, and indicative of user engagement.

In short, ranking factors can be grouped into three buckets:

On-page factors: These include content relevance, keyword use in content, meta data, URL structure, and micro-data (schema)

Off-page factors: These include editorial backlinks to your website and social signals

Authorship: These include author rank and Google+

For those of you who want a deeper download on the ranking factors, I include below the **Periodic Table of SEO Success Factors** (SearchEngineLand.com/seotable), which Danny Sullivan published on Search Engine Land, a place for search engine marketing news.

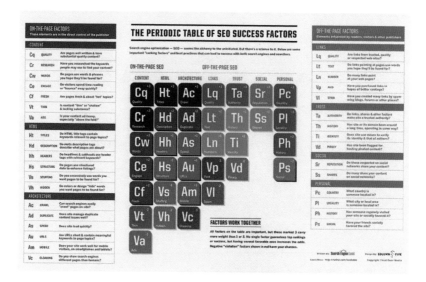

Moz, the premier blog for advanced SEO professionals, reports the shift away from *traditional* ranking factors (including anchor text, exact match domains, meta data, keywords in content) to a deeper analysis of a site's perceived value to users, authorship, structured data, and social signals. Moz's 2013 Google Ranking Factors shows how this shift is playing out:

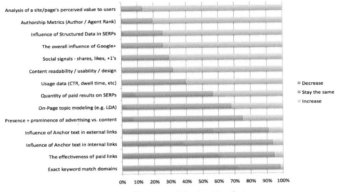

Source: http://moz.com/blog/ranking-factors-

Okay, the graphic above contains a lot of data (SEO nerds love to serve up data by the ton, that's just how they roll). What's important for you to understand at this stage is that all of the ranking trends listed are pointing *away* from the simplistic model of SEO that held a few years ago. Things are changing fast, and as we'll discuss in the next chapter, that's great news – unless you happen to be an SEO spammer, scammer, con man, or outlaw – which brings us to our next section...

The Good, the Bad, and the Ugly About S

Over the years, SEO 'practitioners' have contributed to a m amount of spam and poor quality content on the web.

They broke directories, stuffed content with keywords, spammed the comments on blogs, and bought and traded links in order to game Google's algorithm and push mediocre content toward the top in keyword rankings. Well, it was bad, and sometimes ugly, but it worked! I often call this period the 'Wild West Era' of SEO.

The Wild West Era of SEO

Until 2011, when Google released its first major anti-spam algorithm called Panda, you got on top of Google by buying links and banging out tons of low-quality content.

Those days are over. Recent Google algorithm updates, both Panda and Penguin, rendered most of the old SEO tactics obsolete.

You still need to understand how the search algorithm works to make your content perform on Google or on Facebook's Graph Search. The game change is that, as marketers, we can't be merely concerned about the 'keyword.' Instead, we must optimize our content to relate to 'who' typed it into the search box.

Google's algorithm is essentially a machine trying hard to think like a human. Thus social signals, author authority, and any type of user engagement metrics are becoming a big part of how Google decides that goes on the top.

Don't try to game Google; you cannot. Google has thousands of PhDs from the best engineering schools in the world working for it day in day out. Who are you to challenge it? Rather, focus on the end user – the human being – which is what Google's algorithm is trying to do.

Instead of chasing Google's algorithm, get in front it. Put the user first. Tweet this if you agree with a hashtag #SEOLike5.

In 2014 and beyond, marketers need to align their keyword strategy along the user journey, emphasizing the connection between content and intent (i.e. keyword) through methodical audience profiling, research, and analysis.

The Good: White Hat SEO

The key to SEO success is to focus on quality: quality optimization, quality content, and quality relationships! With quality on your side, both users and the algorithms will be on your side as well.

Quality Optimization. Optimizing your website to help search engine spiders understand what your content is about through on-site technical SEO.

Quality Content. Creating valuable content for your target users that is both shareworthy and linkworthy.

Quality Relationships. Building strong relationships with others in your industry through social media to amplify your content and improve your chances of gaining valuable backlinks to your website.

The Bad: Black Hat SEO

There are many SEO companies and consultants for whom time stopped in 2011. Every second, as we speak, a new business gets sold on $200 hassle-free SEO packages *guaranteed* to get them on the top pages of Google for a number of keywords. Do you really believe in fairy tales? There is no such thing as a free lunch in SEO.

The end result is often more harm than benefit if any of the following practices are involved:

Buying Links. Participating in any type of link schemes or farms. Paying for links is a major violation of Google's terms of service.

Acquiring poor quality links. Creating hundreds of low-quality backlinks manually through directory submissions and commenting. Google knows better; you should too.

Article spinning. Rewriting and publishing low-quality content at scale across the Web. Those links are garbage.

The Ugly: SEO Spam

There are many forms of spam that the shady Internet element of hackers and unethical SEOs thought of over the years. It's a big problem for Google, which is constantly trying to filter its search results from spam.

You can get flagged for spamming and get thrown out of Google's index for practicing any of the below spammy SEO tactics:

Fake accounts, reviews or comments. You can also get sued and fined.

Content spam. These techniques involve keyword stuffing, doorway pages, or hidden or invisible text straight from the 1990s playbook.

Spam blogs. Blogs built on stolen, duplicate content with thousands of useless web pages. These sites exist only for monetization and provide no value to the user.

The Evolution of Google's Secret Sauce

Over the last couple of years, Google has evolved its algorithm from keyword-based search to conversational search to keep pace with the advancement in technology and the expectation of smart users.

In order to combat spam and black hat SEO, Google has also been aggressively targeting abusive websites, leveling the playing field for everyone willing to play by the rules to get a fair chance of ranking.

Panda: End of Low-Quality Content for SEO

In 2011 the old days of the Wild West Era of SEO officially ended. There was a new sheriff in town.

Google's Panda Update is a filter introduced in February 2011 meant to stop sites with poor quality content from working their way into Google's top search results. With this update, content needs to be unique, original, and provide exceptional value to users.

Publishing content just for the heck of traffic is not a good idea anymore. It's a major shift that many small businesses have been slow to realize. If you are buying blog posts for $15 a piece, do you really think Google cares about what you have to say?

Today, you should be more mindful of the things that you publish. Don't make articles just to suck up to search engines; they hate it. You are doing yourself or your clients a disfavor.

Always keep in mind that people want real, useful, quality content – and Google is just trying its best to deliver us what we desire.

Penguin: End of Bad Link Building for SEO

Before the SEO industry regained its footing from Panda's assault on its practices, Google hit them with yet another anti-spam update to its search algorithm.

The Penguin update was aimed at websites that violate Google's Webmaster Guidelines by using now declared black hat SEO techniques used to artificially increase the ranking of a webpage by manipulating the number of backlinks pointing to the page.

While Panda had more to do with low-quality content, Penguin targeted unnatural and paid backlinks.

What makes a bad link profile?

— Links coming from poor quality sites or sites that aren't topically relevant to your niche or business
— Paid links
— Links where the anchor text is overly optimized
— Unnatural, manually created links

Don't try to outsmart Google by buying links under the radar, hoping to get away with your schemes. You may get a couple of quick wins — until you get caught and penalized.

Hummingbird: Search Engine you Can Talk to

With the recent introduction of Hummingbird, Google's search engine now answers, converses, and anticipates. You can now *talk* to your computer and get answers to everything you ask.

Ask conversational search queries like: "What's the closest place to buy the iPhone 5s to my home?" A traditional search engine might focus on finding matches for words — finding a page that says "buy" and "iPhone 5s," for example.

Now, with Hummingbird, Google will focus on the meaning behind the words. It will better understand the actual location of your home, if you've shared that with Google. It might understand that "place" means you want a brick-and-mortar store. It might get that "iPhone 5s" is a particular type of electronic device carried by certain stores. Knowing all of this helps Google go beyond just finding pages with matching words.

Hummingbird introduced gold-rush caliber, yet mostly untapped opportunities for marketers to build their brands and get more traffic. Get in on the action, and reap big benefits.

Early bird gets the worm.

SEO is Not Dead; Black Hat and Spam is

SEO, otherwise known as search engine optimization, has gotten a bad rap over the years. You can see how people feel about SEO by running a simple search.

The "SEO is dead" idea can be debunked by visiting the Webmaster Guidelines for both Google and Bing. Both sites give webmasters tips on how to create a fully optimized website attractive to search engines.

The relationship between Google and SEO is symbiotic. Like the flower and the bee, they benefit from each other. Google wants easy access to discover great content; the role of SEO is to feed that content to Google effectively. Google loves good SEO.

The aim of black hat SEO and spam is to rock the natural order of the World Wide Web. It's based on a parasitic — not a symbiotic — view.

SEO is not dead. At least, quality SEO is not dead. Bad SEO, rife with black hat techniques, is as dead as a dodo.

SEO is no waste of money either, as long as you use a quality, intelligent approach rooted in the 5 Cs you'll learn about in this book. However, if you start buying links from companies selling packages of 1,000 blog and forum comments for $100 or adding every variation of 'dui lawyer' to your homepage, you will likely land in the Google penalty box. Ouch!

Between the loss of search engine visitors and the money you'll have to spend improving your website and backlinks profile, your costs will likely outweigh any temporary profit made through the original schemes.

SEO is a bit overrated in that people make it sound much more complicated than it actually is. The quality, organic SEO that Google loves is not necessarily easy to attain, but with persistent, smart, and hard work described in this book, you can get your SEO game up to snuff.

SEO doesn't have to be scary or daunting. As long as you focus on quality, with the goal of gaining customers, you'll ultimately form a winning SEO strategy. Let's begin.

The 5 Cs of SEO Success

To make it big on the Internet, you need to think big.

Intelligent, spam-free SEO that will get you results in 2014 and beyond can be likened to running an NFL football team. Super Bowl winners are teams of tightly-knit athletes, who all work together like a well-oiled machine to create a championship-caliber team.

SEO is a team effort. You are only as strong as your weakest link. Tweet this if you agree with a hashtag #SEOLike5.

You can compare each of the Cs to a well-organized football team:

Content: Offence
Code: Defense
Credibility: Special Team
Connections: Coaching Staff
Cash: GM

To get ahead of the pack on the crowded Web, you need to play a holistic SEO game. Tweet this if you agree.

In fact, you can tweet anything you find useful in this book with a hashtag #SEOLike5 and I will retweet you. How does that sound for a good SEO strategy?

Well, keep reading. In the Connections chapter of 'SEO Like I'm 5' you will learn more about one of the oldest rules of growth, online or offline: the law of reciprocity.

In a way, **SEO is like an ATM machine: you get out as much as you put in**. How does that sound for another Tweet?

Only by embracing each and all of the 'Cs' will a steady flow of targeted, profitable organic traffic from search engines, blogs, and social media networks be ensured. Neglect any single area and you will fail to maximize your growth online.

The book is designed to walk you through each element of a successful SEO campaign and show you how each C works together, like a band marching in the same direction. I call it the '5 Cs of SEO Success.'

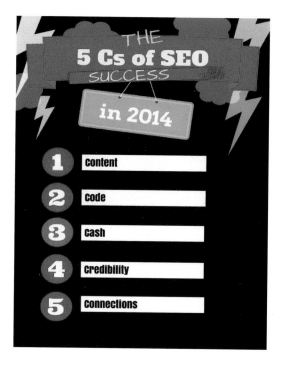

Content. Content is king but only if developed and shared within the right context and targeted to the right audience. Good content is the prerequisite to SEO success. Without it, you will gain no results.

Code. Optimizing your site through technical meta tags and search-friendly web development techniques can be daunting, but it promotes the smart SEO Google and Bing are expecting from you.

Credibility. Learn how to become worth talking about so you can build trusted backlinks to your website using smart content strategies and outreach techniques.

Connections. Use social media sites to establish connections with experts and influencers. Publish native content on emerging social platforms such as SlideShare, Reddit, and Medium to reach new audiences.

Cash. Put the user first, but identify your monetization strategy at the outset. Always collect leads, which will help you make cash after you've developed trust and authority online. Trust me: it's the best way to get rich online.

Before You Begin

I thought it would be helpful to create a resource page for the 'absolute' starters who need to build their online presence from scratch. This page can be a place you can always come back to when you decide to build a website for your business.

One of the most common questions I get asked when I deliver SEO workshops and talks is which software to use to build a website or a blog.

One of the most common limitations to online growth is when you get yourself locked into a platform that cannot be customized or updated with ease. So, let's get things right from the get-go.

If it's not easy, you must be doing something wrong. Tweet this if you agree with a hashtag #SEOLike5.

I always try to stay on top of the technology, constantly testing multiple tools and emerging platforms.

Here is a hassle-free starter's toolbox I wish I had known about when I was starting out online. By the way, the companies I mention do not pay me. There are no sponsored mentions in this book. Just the good stuff that I tested over the years.

Hosting and Domain: GoDaddy. One of the key values of using GoDaddy is their amazing customer support. You can call the support line and speak to a real person in minutes who'll walk you step-by-step through any technical challenge. If you are not a techie, go with GoDaddy. Make sure you search for 'GoDaddy Coupons' in Google to save a couple bucks every time you buy a domain.

The easiest way to start a website is to buy your domain, host it through GoDaddy, and use the included Wordpress widget below to build it.

Website/Blogging Platform: WordPress. WordPress combines ease of use with nearly unlimited customization and multiple available SEO plugins. For example, if you install the **Yoast** plugin, you will be able to implement all the SEO tags with ease, without ever having to learn a line of HTML. I moved from Blogger to WordPress a couple year ago and it took my blogging game to the next level.

I use **WooThemes** (**Canvas** template), which provides a set of simple tools that anyone with basic computer knowledge can use to build and customize a website from scratch.

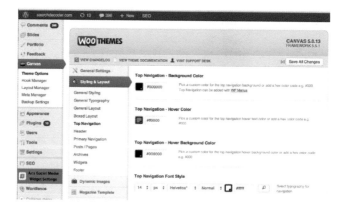

Email Marketing: AWeber. One of my biggest regrets when I started blogging is how long I waited before collecting emails to build my newsletter list. AWeber is a fantastic tool to help you easily create and embed email opt-in forms and manage your email marketing campaigns, all in one place. I use it specifically in the right rail of my blog.

If you are into testing and analytics, you can connect AWeber with Unbounce for better results.

Analytics: Google Analytics. If you are a small business or a blogger, Google Analytics will satisfy most of your website analytics and tracking needs. You can easily measure your website visits and conversions, advertising ROI, as well as track traffic from video and social networking sites and applications. Make sure to sync Analytics with Google Adwords and Webmaster Tools to get full tracking functionality.

Webmaster Tools. Both Google and Bing offer Webmaster Tools without any charge. They provide a convenient way for webmasters and bloggers to check their status in the search engines' index, examine the keywords that searchers are using to access their sites, check for any site errors such as broken links, and other useful features. Make sure you link Webmaster Tools to your Analytics package to get the most complete picture of your site/blog's performance.

Part 1: CONTENT

Content marketing and SEO often live in separate silos, but they're two sides of the same coin. Tweet this if you agree with a hashtag #SEOLike5.

With about 160 million blogs online, and 4 billion hours of video being watched each month on YouTube, there is a huge opportunity for brands to connect with their consumers via compelling content.

The problem is that most content marketing initiatives underperform because big creative ideas are rarely integrated with a data-driven, performance-based approach.

In a recent post on Content Marketing Institute, "Content Marketing vs. SEO: The Truth Behind a Ridiculous Debate," Barry Feldman of Feldman Creative rightly noted:

"You could make the case that SEO is content marketing. Search engine optimization is a misnomer anyway. It seems to suggest you optimize the search engine. Clearly, you cannot and do not. You optimize online content."

In a world where 80 percent of consumers search online for a product before purchasing it, the goal of content marketers is to not only plan and create content, but also to find a way to make it more discoverable in top search engine results.

Great content can go unnoticed without SEO, while SEO-led content can do poorly because it is not compelling. That's why brands need a holistic approach to content marketing that emphasizes creative and performance equally.

The Magic of Content Marketing

Have you heard about Buffer? It's a social media platform that allows content sharing automation, like HootSuite.

Buffer got really hot on the Internet when it launched, growing from 0 to 100K users in nine months. That's pretty good growth hacking if you ask me.

How did one of the most recognizable social media tools manage to scale so quickly?

Facebook ads? TV ads during the Super Bowl? Banners? Black magic?

None of the above. The answer is smart content marketing and SEO.

Buffer's co-founder, Leo Wildrich, used a strong guest blogging strategy, writing and posting insightful blog posts all over the Web.

Google 'buffer guest blogging' to learn more about specific tactics Leo used to get such amazing results. Guest blogging is also covered extensively by a content marketing guru, Brian Honigman, in the Credibility section of book.

How to become someone worth talking about?

Being interesting isn't just about learning how to become a good conversationalist. You need stories to tell.

I realized it early in life. In every job and at every stage of my life I had unique content that gave me an edge, and eventually propelled me ahead of the pack. You need to offer your network or your company something of value to differentiate yourself.

How do you become someone worth talking to, or even better, worth talking about?

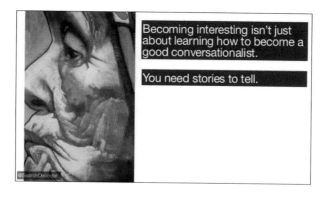

Your content is your work portfolio. It's your differentiator. It's what makes you stand out among the timid masses no matter who you are and where you are from.

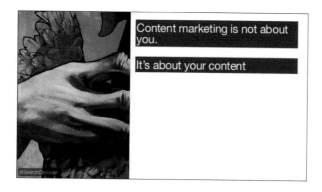

It shows you're interested and involved in the world around you. It shows your expertise. It's what makes you interesting in life, and on the Internet.

It's the message that will make your personal brand stand out, attracting others to become part of your network.

Keith Ferrazzi, author of 'Never Eat Alone,' describes content as 'a cause, an idea, trend, or skill — the unique subject matter on which you are the authority.' He explains further:

"Content involves a specialized knowledge. It's knowing what you have that others don't. It's your expertise. Being known is just notoriety. But being known for something is entirely different. That's respect. You have to believe in something for people to believe in you."

It's old news that every business or individual is a media company, yet so many are slow to embrace the new reality.

In order to keep up, both businesses and individuals need to transform. If we are going to survive and thrive in the new digital economy, we need to choose ourselves, explains James Altucher, author of Amazon self-published hit 'Choose Yourself:'

"The world is changing. Markets have crashed. Jobs have disappeared. Industries have been disrupted and are being remade before our eyes. Everything we aspired to for 'security,' everything we thought was 'safe,' no longer is: College. Employment. Retirement. Government. It's all crumbling down. No longer is someone coming to hire you, to invest in your company, to sign you, to pick you. It's on you to make the most important decision in your life: **Choose Yourself**."

The ethic of the 'Choose Yourself era' is to not depend on those stifling trends that are defeating you. Instead, build your own platform/brand/online presence. Have faith and confidence in yourself, instead of a jury-rigged system, and define success by your own terms.

Whoever you are and whatever you do, your number one job is to build your **credibility** on the Internet through **native content** and **social connections**.

The Internet — search engines, blogs, and social media — have democratized marketing on the Internet. The playground has never been better for small business to compete with big brands and individuals to bypass the middlemen.

New tools and economic forces have emerged to make it possible for businesses to tell stories through content and individuals to create art (i.e. content) and make millions, without relaying on big record labels, corporations, publishing houses, or governments to pick them.

You've seen those trends with your own eyes. Your neighbors and friends have founded successful businesses on the Internet with no money, investors, or blown-out business plans.

Millions of people around the world have become **solopreneurs**, making enough money online to live a happy Internet lifestyle.

I recently read Hugh Howey's self-published post apocalyptic sci-fi thriller "Wool," which sold more than half a million copies and generated more than 5,260 Amazon reviews. Hugh raked in more than a million dollars in royalties and sold the film rights to Alien producer Ridley Scott...and all that happened before Simon & Schuster released the book.

"I had made seven figures on my own, so it was easy to walk away," says Hugh Howey, 37, a college dropout who worked as a yacht captain, a roofer, and a bookseller before he started self-publishing. "I thought, 'How are you guys going to sell six times what I'm selling now?'" the WSJ reported.

The conventional methods for content distribution are being disrupted before our own eyes. Tweet this if you agree with a hashtap #SEOLike5.

In another example, Alex Day, a DIY, YouTube sensation, with no record label, released his latest album in the UK the same day Justin Timberlake did. Alex Day beat him.

Here is how Alex, a 23-year-old unsigned musician, explains his success (via JamesAltucher.com):

"I started in 2006 with 30 subscribers on YouTube. I began talking to the audience that was there and making videos directly for them and replying to comments, but I never saw it as a 'fan base'—I mainly just figured we were all bored kids. I really don't feel the need to gig when I can reach my audience online and hit everyone at once, all over the world, and not exclude anybody, which a tour doesn't do."

Personal branding is branding; and you need to humanize your business through storytelling to succeed in SEO.

Tom Peters, a best-selling writer on business management practices, best known for "In Search of Excellence," wrote:

"Regardless of age, regardless of position, regardless of the business we happen to be in, all of us need to understand the importance of branding. We are the CEOs of our own companies: Me Inc. To be successful today, our most important job is to be head marketer of the brand called YOU."

As a marketer and an entrepreneur, I am keenly aware that perception drives reality. However, the times have changed. No longer can you put up a promo video on YouTube or publish an article on Forbes with the help of a ghostwriter and a PR agency, and expect to be Internet cool. It needs to be YOU. You need to be authentic and act like a user.

Your content needs to become the guiding star of your online presence, helping you establish credentials and build relationships with others. It will open doors you have never imagined to be unlocked.

Your content — provided that it is (1) great/compelling/relevant, (2) original/unique/authentic, and (3) native to the platform you are using — will attract more and more people to you and your message, and you will stand out in an increasingly cluttered world.

If you choose yourself and persist, you will find it easier to win new friends and have more say in what you do, how you live, and where you work.

Your content establishes your worth, both in life and on the Internet. Google understands this, and you'd better catch up or become an obsolete relic of the past.

Content articulates what you have to offer, why you are unique, and it gives a reason for others to be interested in you. Keith Ferrazi makes it plain:

"By making the effort, you can break the glass ceiling by expanding people view of your capability. It's the email you read because of who it's from. It's the employee who gets the cool projects."

Every day. Seven days a week. I strive to live by the principles I described above.

Every day, I read and learn from writers such as Keith Ferrazzi, James Altucher, Austin Kleon, Seth Godin, Gary Vaynerchuk, and many more. I can't thank them enough for sharing their experience and knowledge.

I am a bootstrapping dreamprenuer. For life.

I hope you are too. It's a fun and rewarding way to live.

Winning Content Marketing Tools and Strategies

Content marketing and content strategy are two different animals, yet the terms are often confused and used interchangeably. Getting things right at the outset is key.

What is Content Marketing?

Think of content marketing as being similar to **baking a cake for a party**. Content marketing is the actual creation and sharing of content to attract and engage a defined audience.

If you think of baking a cake and bringing the cake to a party, you can see how content marketing works. The cake either disappears in an instant or nobody touches it. You measure your success by how much cake is left after the party.

What is Content Strategy?

Content strategy is similar to **running a bakery**. It's the planning and creation of scalable and repeatable content with a built-in audience. The content itself is both shareworthy and linkworthy because you built it with this objective in mind, targeting niche topics and audiences.
Visualize yourself running a successful bakery. Each loaf of bread, donut, cupcake, or baguette you bake is similar to the various types of content like e-books, blog posts, YouTube videos, and podcasts you create.

You need to manage your inventory. What type of content do you need to 'bake' more of? What doesn't sell? What do people ask for?

You'd use your bakery's blenders and ovens to create baked goods in a way that's similar to creating content. The bakery manager, or someone in charge, directs a workforce to service customers and promote the business in the same way that a content strategist manages a team and builds a promotional plan.

Content Marketing is Like a Healthy Heartbeat

A healthy heartbeat registers a slow and steady contrast of beats and rests. It never stops beating. The objective of content strategy is to build an always-on content marketing operation that is constantly pulsing out a steady flow of content.

Daily content includes provocative conversation on social media. You should also be curating thought leadership content by sharing industry news and trends. Every day. Use scheduling tools like Hootsuite and Buffer to help you manage multiple social networks.

Weekly content includes shareable micro-content such as blog posts, graphics, memes, and videos. Micro-content helps you make a series of smaller hits with a heavy cumulative impact if you are consistent.

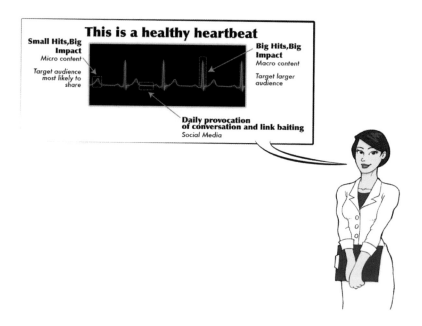

Monthly content includes your macro-content, such as a marketing campaign, a launch of a new product, an ebook, or a white paper. Publishing branded content or hiring PR agencies to spread the word helps target larger audiences to leverage your brand presence quickly and support your SEO objectives. Macro-content is a collaborative effort, so as an SEO practitioner you need to play well with others.

Mike King, SEO engineer and content strategist, compares content marketing to building cars:

Building websites without a well thought out content and SEO strategy is like building a car with no engine. Tweet this if you agree with a hashtag #SEOLike5.

A Ferrari without an engine cannot move. Content is what powers your website, not the design or color of your fonts.

Are sites such as Reddit, Wikipedia, Amazon or Craigslist pretty? Check them out. While they look all right, the graphics are not what they are famous for.

Here's the Alexa ranking of the top websites in the US (http://www.alexa.com/topsites/countries/US):

#1 Google
#5 Amazon
#6 Wikipedia
#10 Craigslist
#18 Reddit

So, how did Craigslist and Reddit become two of the most successful websites on the Internet?

The webmasters managing those sites spend little time filling up the white space with creative designs. They are too busy banging out amazing content, building communities, optimizing technical tags,

55

and using every bit of data to provide the best possible user experience.

However, 90% of a typical web development budget and most of the work effort is spent on design, creative, and copywriting. I kid you not.

The core building blocks of Internet success — SEO, content strategy, blog strategy, analytics, user experience/UX — are often treated as an afterthought. The specialists in those areas tend to be detached from the business strategy.

As an SEO practitioner and content marketing consultant, I often get calls from clients with the exact same issue: "I just built a new beautiful website, can you **SEO it** for me??? I need to be on top of Google because I need to ramp up organic search traffic pronto. Here is the list of keywords. Can you help me?"

My answer is always the same: "Nope. Good luck."

Content Marketing 101

First, you need to build your content library beyond your homepage, product pages, and landing pages for paid media.

If all you have on your website is a collection of landing pages, you need to start blogging, building web pages that solve user problems, and build visual content such as videos and infographics that users 'actually' want to share, talk about, and link to.

Don't get me wrong: your product pages are key for SEO. However, in order to build your visibility in Google, you need more content on your website to increase your domain authority, Page Rank, and rank on your keywords.

Most businesses do this by creating informative blog posts, but keep in mind that blog content is not the end all of a smart content creation campaign.

Play to Your Strengths

Always play to your strengths. Don't jump into building infographics because you heard that they are good for SEO if you are not a designer or cannot afford one. Start with a meticulous self-evaluation.

Ask yourself the following at the outset: Do you have design and writing skills? Who will be in charge of content? Does the team have time for all this?

Choosing the right content medium helps you to resonate with your ideal target audience and be your best self.

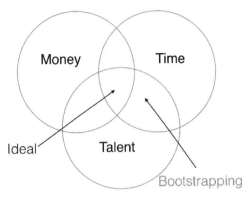

If you are starting out, begin by choose a medium which best complements your talents.

Text Content Tools

Maybe you prefer to type away in front of your laptop for hours on end. If so, create text blog posts to woo your audience with great storytelling.

Medium.com is a great place for beginner writers to start off getting feedback and traffic. Medium has social media widgets that will help you spread your stories to your audience.

Other places where it's easy to start include LinkedIn and Quora, where you can post questions, comments, and blog posts. Your own blog should be the cornerstone of your SEO strategy. However, if you are just starting out, write on platforms with a bigger audience than yours that will allow your content to get more eyeballs.

If writing is not your forte, hire employees that can write well, or arrange to get the budget required to hire a good writer. As you grow your writing skills, consider e-books, guides, and guest posting on online publications.

Source and co-create content through interviews, Q&As, curation, and reblogging. More on those tactics later in this section.

Video Content Tools

Do you like to ham it up in front of the camera? Create video blog posts on YouTube. Learn basic video production and editing to make your videos look professional. Don't put up video clips from your iPhone.

Video strategies include getting in front of the camera and talking about a particular topic, recording screencasts and webinars, conducting interviews and Google+ Hangouts, and creating animated videos.

If you are not great in front of the camera, hire an actor. You can find plenty of amateurs who will record a video for you for $5, using sites like **Fiverr.com**. Just send them a script with what to say. I did just that to promote my bootstrap marketing content.

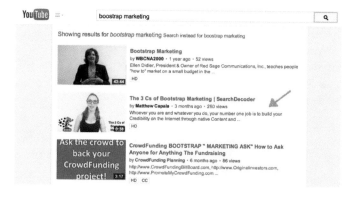

Visual content, including videos, are an important part of your SEO strategy. Recall the composition of the Google SERP?

Leverage video platforms such as YouTube and Vimeo for video content promotion and distribution. And don't forget to embed your videos on your website and on social networks.

Photo Content Tools

If you are a skilled photographer, consider using Pinterest, Flickr and Instagram to expand your blogging presence. You can also use Creative Commons to offer your photos for bloggers to use if they give you credit (and link back to you). Here is a good photo content hack:

#1 Just walk around your city, or, when you travel, take pictures of the things that inspire you with your high-res smartphone camera. Upload the photos you like to **Imgur.com**, an image hosting and sharing platform. Best of all, Imgur is free.

#2 Use your own image bank for other forms of content you put out, such as decks, blog posts and on social media. If others use your content, track them down and ask for credit with a backlink to your site.

You can also approach bloggers and offer them your photo content for free with a credit attribution and backlink to your website.

You see, bloggers always need quality, rights-free photo content. They are often bootstrapping just like you. The best practice is to use at least three images per blog post, including a strong 'featured image' that will be assigned to your social media post headlines.

Use photo sourcing tools such as **PhotoPin.com** to find free images for your content. Always give credit to the photographer/author following the instructions on the site. That's how a content creator gets a credit (and a link); failing to provide credit is stealing. You can also leverage platforms like PhotoPin to share your own images.

Do not just copy images off Google Image search. Most of them are not rights-free.

If you have a bigger budget, use sites like iStockPhoto, Getty Images, AP Images, or Corbis.

Audio Content Tools

Some bloggers prefer to be on the interviewing side of the microphone. Consider publishing podcasts, using tools like **Stitcher** and iTunes for delivery.

I am a BIG fan of podcasting, which is growing very quickly due to the growth of mobile use and introduction of the smart car. I listen to James Altucher, one of the biggest names in the podcasting game. James does a daily podcast, which can be overkill for many content creators, but he understands the power of 'compounding.'

I am kicking off my own podcast, **Solopreneur Camp**, in the Fall of 2014. Get on my mailing list (searchdecoder.com/newsletter) for updates. You don't want to miss it.

A good podcasting hack is to use tools such as **SpeechPad** to get a transcript of your audio content for a small fee so that you can turn it into blog post content.

You can do a Skype or Google Hangout interview for video content, use it on **iTunes** as audio content, and finally use it on your blog as text content. Compound. Compound. And compound some more.

Graphics Content Tools

Designers would be wise to go the Infographics or meme route.

Memes work well on **Reddit** and Infographics on **Visual.ly**. Data visualization lets you visually convey the meaning of big volumes of data in a way that users will be eager to share and bloggers to embed.

You can use plenty of low-cost graphics sourcing tools, such as **Elance.com** or **99Designs.com**. My personal favorite is **Fiverr.com**, where you can buy graphic gigs for as low as $5. In fact I used Fiverr to create a lot of graphics for the book, working with Adzakeal from Malaysia, who I think did a really good job.

A lot of people still don't believe that I paid only $5 for each graphic you see in this book. A creative agency would charge you hundreds or thousands of dollars. Proof below.

Spam Warning: Do not use any of the $5 SEO gigs on Fiverr. Most of these gigs are garbage that can do more harm than good, and are what I refer to this my book as the Bad and the Ugly of SEO (i.e black hat techniques and spam). You do not, and can not, buy hundreds of quality backlinks for $5. You know better!

Rather, develop a creative brief and 'gig it out 'to the crowd on

Fiverr. If you are a bigger brand, you can also use **SpringLeap.com**, a creative crowdsourcing marketplace for Fortune 500 brands.

The key to success in crowdsourcing content is to find the right partner and communicate your needs clearly.

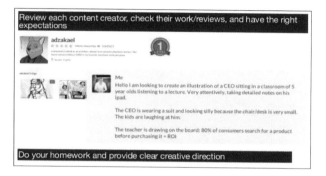

For $5 you will not get the creative brief; only the execution. So make sure you clearly explain what you want in advance.

I use **Canva.com** a lot, and created a bunch of graphics for this book using this tool. It's awesome. You get hundreds of free templates you can easily customize to create awesome content: posters, flyers, presentations, social media profile headers, visual quotes, business cards, social media posts, blog graphics, and more.

Don't take content marketing too seriously. You want to provide **infotainment**; not just dry information or just entertainment, says Gary Vaynerchuk, best-selling author of "Jab, Jab, Jab, Right Hook."

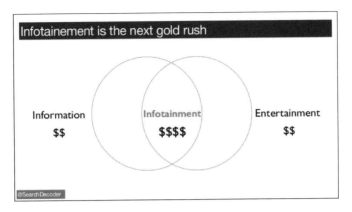

Use memes to jazz up your your visual content strategies and let your creative juices flow. I use **MemeGenerator.net** for all my memes, like this one:

The importance of picking the right set of tools and strategies that best fit your situation (time, talent, money) at the outset cannot be overstated. The more content types you create and cross-optimize, the better your online visibility will be (AKA the compounding effect).

Before we move on, I wanted to provide you with a solid summary of infographic creation tools.

Infographic Toolbox

Easel.Ly. Easel.Ly is a theme-based web app for creating data visualizations and graphics. The best feature is drag and drop navigation that makes creating, editing and customizing intuitive and easy.

Piktochart. Piktochart is an simple and intuitive online tool for creating high resolution infographics and charts as part of any web marketing strategy. They offer six free themes with a good selection of graphics and the ability to use present graphics and templates.

Visual.ly. Visual.ly is an online platform for creating infographics and diagrams that integrate seamlessly with social networks. They offer a community Marketplace that connects designers and motion graphics artists who specialize in the development of more customized infographics.

Infogr.am. Infogr.am is a web-based tool with a user-friendly interface and a selection of great pre-designed themes for creating charts using real data. They offer 31 chart options that allow you to add your own video, maps and imagery as well as the ability to embed it quickly to a website or blog post.

Reposting Published Content

Repurposing involves taking one type of content and transforming it into another form. Repurposing content maximizes the great power of compounding.

Each time you create one piece of content, you can transform this content into another piece.

For example, if you create a video, have it transcribed into a blog post. Or if you create a blog post, turn it into a script that can form the basis of a podcast. I use **SpeechPad** for my transcripts.

You also want to build a large volume of one content type and convert this content into another type. For example, you can repackage a series of blog posts into an e-book. Or if you record a series of interviews on video or podcast, you can later release the audio-only versions of those interviews as podcasts.

In action: I repurposed one of my NYU class lectures that was conducted in an interactive Q&A panel format with Mike King and his iAcquire team, into video content, which I then transcribed into a comprehensive blog post. In this post I included embedded SlideShare decks, infographics, and various resources to maximize value for the reader.

The post received over 200 shares, 17 comments, a 35 page authority score, and 12 root domain backlinks, at the time when I was just getting started blogging, which propelled my blog to a much better place on Google's ranking map.

SearchDecoder.com/content-marketing-tips-and-seo-strategies/

Another way to repurpose and repost is to publish content on your own blog first so that Google can crawl and index it, assigning you the authorship value. Then you can post this content on social media networks that offer publishing tools, such as **Linkedin** or **Medium**, so that your connections can get push notifications through those platforms. Use with caution (no more than twice a week).

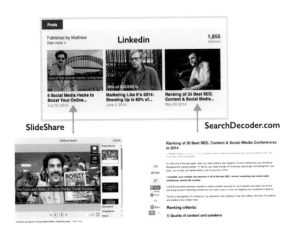

In fact, my very strategy for the book content you are reading right now is **rooted in the principle of compounding**.

Here's my game plan:

#1 Blog content, interviews, guest posts
#2 Free e-books and guides
#3 Amazon Kindle
#4 Paperback Book
#5 Audio Book (looking for an amazing voice-over, any takers?)
#6 Class on Udemy
#7 Paid speaking engagements
#8 Consulting gigs

Repurposing helps you get more out of your content development investment, spreading your passive income streams into different audiences across many platforms. You can appeal to people across a wide range of marketing channels and improve your linking for a wider audience.

You Need Data-Driven Content Marketing

If you engage in content marketing and don't have personas developed and validated by quantitative research, start over. You need to make content decisions based on data in order to build content with a built-in ROI. Measure and test everything.

Great content that is optimized and targeted towards pre-defined personas pulls your audience in naturally, so don't get too pushy.

You want to limit choice and drive a user through your content towards your calls-to-action, aligning with user personas, but avoiding overselling. Rand Fishkin, the founder and CEO of Moz, puts it best: "A nudge is mightier than a sword."

Create or Curate?

Original, high-quality content created by humans is especially prized by searchers, search engines, and social network services. But not every piece of content you publish has to be original work. There's a place for "curated content" in your content strategy.

Like a museum curator, a content curator doesn't paint the pictures on a museum's walls, but adds value to a museum goer's experience by interpreting "what those paintings mean", and making wise decisions about the works that should be in a given gallery at a given time. Here's Lisha Kapish, my former student at NYU who's curated a lot of great content as a member of Inbound Marketing Clinic, sharing her views on how content curation can add value to your content strategy:

What is Content Curation

Next is a contribution by Lisha Kapish, my former NYU student, which was originally published on SearchDecoder.com, as a part of the Inbound Marketing Clinic project that I started within M.S. in Integrated Marketing program at NYU SCPS.

According to author and non-profit social media expert Beth Kanter: **Content curation** is the process of sorting through the vast amounts of content on the web and presenting it in a meaningful and organized way around a specific theme.

Think of it like panning for gold – where you have to look through piles of dirt and rock, examining each little piece in an attempt to find that 'golden nugget.'

A **content curator** is someone who carefully selects relevant pieces of information and transforms this into content that's shareable. The content curator identifies the theme and provides the context that makes the content relevant.

According to Clay Shirky, author and NYU Professor, "Curation comes up when search stops working. Curation comes up when people realize that it isn't just about information seeking, it's also about synchronizing a community."

The essential difference in content curation is that there is a human being doing the sifting, sorting, arranging, and publishing.

What is the Role of Content Curation?

The Internet has become a place where massive amounts of information and data are being generated every day. Through the proliferation of the web, anyone has the ability to be a content curator, however you might have heard the following saying in the SEO world:

Not all content is created equal...this is certainly true.

A content curator offers high value to anyone looking for quality content because finding information and making sense of it requires time, patience, and focus. This is where the role of brands as content curators comes in. Content curation gives brands the ability to become thought leaders in their industry/category, build their audience, and create scale through their content marketing efforts.

The Content Curation Process

Content Aggregation. Collecting content that is relevant to your brand or the brand themes created. An RSS feed is a simple example of a content aggregation tool that pulls information from various sources.

Content Selection. Sorting through the content that has been collected by analyzing and selecting the best and most relevant content that can be used according to your brand or brand themes.

Content Contextualization. Showcasing the best 'golden nuggets' of content to your audience in a format they can easily digest. The value is added here through the 'contextualizing' of the content. It is essential that your brand does this in a distinct and ownable way.

Content Curation Tools

There are some great content curation tools available on the web to help with one or more steps in the process:

BagTheWeb: This service helps users curate Web content. For any topic, create, collect, publish, and share any content from the Web.

List.ly: This is a tool to help bloggers and brands curate, crowdsource, and engage readers via live embedded content inside blog posts.

Scoop.it: This lets professionals share important ideas with the right audiences, giving them an opportunity to create and maintain a meaningful Web presence.

Curata: Curata lets you easily find, organize, and share relevant content for your business.

Storify: Storify helps to make sense of the content people post on social media. You can curate the most important voices and turn them into stories.

Netvibes.com: Netvibes provides a real-time social dashboard.

How to Measure Content Performance?

Experts feel that if you can't measure anything, then why market it? Establishing goals is one of the most important starting elements of a digital marketing campaign. Without an accurate benchmark to measure efforts against, the true value of a marketing campaign may never be understood.

Being a digital marketer that has worked both in-house and on the agency side, I've experienced many different scenarios that boil down to five main categories of success metrics.

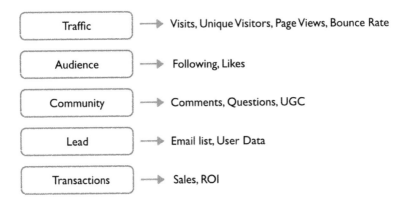

Traffic. How many people read your article (Page views)? How long did they spend on it (longer usually equals better). Did they "bounce" back or go forward into your site? All of these answers are available in your site analytics package (we recommend Google Analytics, which is free).

Audience. Are people following what you post? Do they like it? Do they forward (Retweet) it?

Community. How engaged is your online community with what you post? Does your content stimulate discussions, comments, and perhaps even mashups and other instances of UCG (User-Generated Content)?

Leads. Are people interested enough in your professional opinion and credentials to actually ask you to help them with a business problem?

Transactions. If you're selling goods and service online, you'll know whether your content is stimulating orders and sales by examining your e-commerce numbers.

Creating a Killer Content Strategy

A strong content strategy should answer the following questions:

What are your content goals? Do you want more conversions, more social engagement, or more links?

Who is your audience? If your goal is to increase conversions, then you must write for your specific audience.

Who will develop your content for you? Will you do it yourself, delegate it to your employees, or outsource the process?

How often do you want to publish new content? And do you have the resources to fulfill the commitment to daily blog posts, weekly podcasts, or monthly videos?

How will you promote your content to reach a targeted audience? Will you depend on organic social reach, pay for advertising, or dedicate time to blogger outreach?

How will you measure your results to ensure that your content strategy is meeting your goals?

Your content strategy will begin to materialize as you answer the questions above.

User Personas: Whom Are You Marketing to?

Your content strategy should start with creating user personas for individuals whose vibe matches your content.

There is no expert on the topic of developing personas more knowledgeable than Mike King, who put together the most comprehensive resource on the subject on the Moz blog: "Personas: The Art and Science of Understanding the Person Behind the Visit."

There's been much talk about various marketing channels, but not much talk about understanding who you're marketing to.

This is the most crucial step that can help any marketing campaign (digital or traditional) hit the mark.

iPULLRANK

@iPullRank

He describes personas as **a method of market segmentation** wherein we collect a combination of qualitative and quantitative data to build archetypes of the members of our target audience. In other words, we take data to tell a predictive story about our users based on past behaviors and attributes.

How you can you create effective content without first gaining a deep understanding of that audience? You might as well be writing with your eyes closed like this guy.

iPULLRANK

@iPullRank

To make it plain and simple, visualize your ideal website visitor. Based on behaviors and other characteristics, segment your ideal visitors into user personas. Give your personas names and attach look-alike pictures to humanize your content strategy.

STYLISH SMURFETTE
Stylish Smurfette got all high-end fashion on us, dying her hair blonde, wearing Diane von Smurfstenburg dresses and Christian Smurfboutin shoes. She's more likely to be found at high end establishments, but only goes out when invited. Stylish Smurfette would rather be shopping than go to a music night spot. She's all about convenience over supporting her local community. Stylish Smurfette likes to see and be seen.

SCUZZY SMURFETTE
She shops at second hand stores before it was in style. No, really. Scuzzy Smurfette goes to open mics and loves to be around music. She enjoys vintage vinyl records and playing with her rescue cat. The Scuzzy Smurfette is a bit of a couch surfer who frequents SmurfBN3 and eats at Baker Smurf's restaurant rather than the big chains. You guessed it; Scuzzy Smurfette is a persona based on the female Hipster Millenial cohort.

Personas are archetypal representations of actual people in your target audience. Depending on whose model you follow they typically include a user story, user needs, engagement insights. They are often given alliterated names and have a quote that personifies them quickly.

iPULLRANK   @iPullRank

Maximizing Your Content Potential

To succeed at content marketing, you've got to find a way to serve up high-quality content on a regular basis. This can be a major challenge. Creativity and inspiration aren't linear and predictable, and writer's block is always a danger. But the last thing you want to do is wind up in a 'content gulch.'

One very helpful approach comes from Didit's Ana Raynes, whose group must serve up many pieces of content each week over multiple channels. Using a tool called **XMind**, she uses an approach she calls 'the Spider method.'

The Spider Method

As your content efforts grow, you will start thinking about productivity and scalability. You want to make sure you are maximizing your much-coveted resources. For some people reading this, you may be the only resource available for your business. If this is the case, the spider will especially help you.

The 'Spider,' as we refer to it at Didit, is a **mind map**. A mind map is a diagram that helps to visually organize information. There are many mind map tools out there. After some heavy research I found **XMind** to be the best product for our marketing needs.

Moving on, the way we organize our mind map is as follows:

What are we trying to achieve with this content? Start with the end goal in mind. For us it's primarily more leads.

How do we get more leads? We need people to sign up for our newsletter so that we can start them travelling through the sales funnel.

How do we get people activated in the sales funnel? We need them to download something of value.

What is the best way to provide something of value? A white paper or e-book.

So our goal is to write a white paper or e-book, because by doing so, we will garner more emails that will be activated through our sales funnel, potentially leading to more sales leads.

The end result of your Spider Method content strategy planning should look like this:

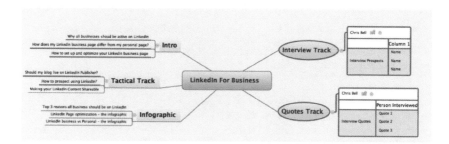

For this example, our goal will be a LinkedIn for business e-book.

What topics to do we want to cover?

The standard topics for us are:

Introduce the product, service, or tool through blog topics such as a benefits list, a comparison list, or a how-to.

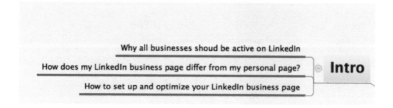

Next, we create more **tactical content** for our most advanced readers. This will be more relevant to your topic of interest. However, you can see how the subject matter is not for the beginner still seeking to set up a LinkedIn page. Keep your audience in mind when you set up your tactical track for the spider arm. You want to show your expertise and encourage prospects to reach out without confusing them with overly granular content.

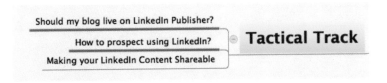

Now we move to our **Interview track**. This is probably the most important track. Here you will identify bloggers and influencers within your field that can provide expert advice. When you interview experts, influencers and bloggers, they will most likely drive traffic to your post via social media. Remember, even if they choose not to promote your post, there is still value.

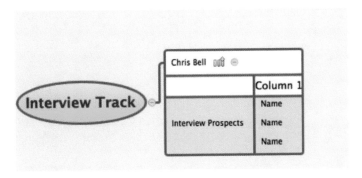

We have seen through Google Analytics that posts that were not promoted via the influencer were picked up and shared by their fans. You never know where the traffic or pick up will come from when you broaden your net.

Pro Tip: Take a few minutes to research the authority of your bloggers and influencers by looking at their social media profiles, blogs, and/or website ranking on Alexa.com. You want to make sure that you are choosing people with a broad reach in order to expand your visibility.

The next step is probably the easiest. With so many great free designing tools like **Canva** and **PicMonkey**, anyone can create compelling images with little or no design skills. The fourth arm to the spider method is quotes. Here is an example from our Pinterest board:

What you want to do here is convert your influencer advice from arm 3 into visual quotes, which are low-effort, high-engagement social and blog content. Images can be shared at a larger scale than written content by creating quotes that can be shared through social and on your website. By doing this, you are creating more opportunity for your audience and your influencer's audience to see your content.

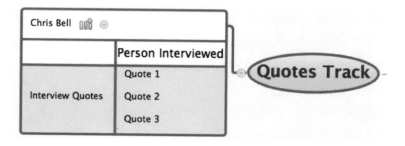

Note: I intentionally left the names of the people we interviewed and the quotes blank because we have yet to publish the above content. But if you visit our blog Didit.com, a lot of the content presented in this book might have already filled up.

Last we have the **Infographics** track. Again, no real design skills are needed. You can use simple-to-use infographic generators, such as Vizualize, Eazel.ly or Piktochart, to create powerful infographics for your content. Here is an example of an infographic our team put together.

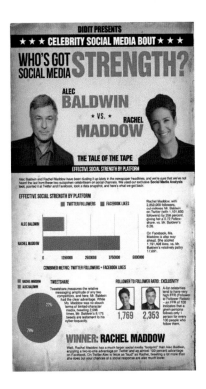

Take a look at how we repurpose the content from the intro leg and the tactical leg for the infographics section. You do not need to rattle your head for new content; work with what you have to expedite and maximize your efforts.

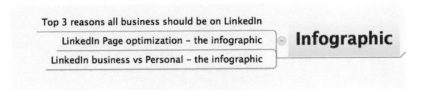

Your spider should now look like the one below. Of course, you can continue to add on to the spider but this will ensure that you are posting at least one piece of content a week for some time.

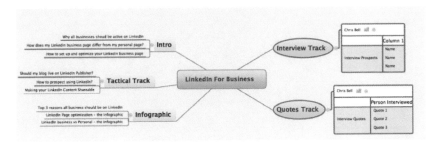

Becoming a Rockstar Blogger

Joseph Campbell, one of the world's most respected methodologists, gave us a simple yet profound proposition for life: **Follow your bliss.**

The Internet and social media tools enable anyone to follow her or his bliss and make money. For the first time in the history of humankind, you can turn a hobby into an online business by bootstrapping from the comfort of your couch (or – like my good friend Ryan Biddulph – a village somewhere in Thailand).

Do you know how many blog posts are written today? Check out **Worldometers**' counter that provides real-time data on the total number of blog posts published each day in the world (powered by Technorati). In short, millions.

	Society & Media	
1,417,150	New book titles published this year	info ⌄
363,491,023	Newspapers circulated today	info ⌄
474,820	TV sets sold worldwide today	info ⌄
3,692,324	Cellular phones sold today	info ⌄
$ 134,298,230	Money spent on videogames today	info ⌄
2,941,072,749	Internet users in the world	info ⌄
150,953,671,792	Emails sent today	info ⌄
2,568,220	Blog posts written today	info ⌄
462,588,609	Tweets sent today	info ⌄
2,806,836,640	Google searches today	info ⌄

10 Habits of Rockstar Bloggers

#1 Rockstar bloggers chase their passions, not dollars.

#2 Rockstar bloggers believe in themselves.

#3 Rockstar bloggers play the long-term game.

#4 Rockstar bloggers embrace failure as a part of the game.

#5 Rockstar bloggers are more interested in others than in themselves.

#6 Rockstar bloggers are very hard workers.

#7 Rockstar bloggers respond to every tweet and comment.

#8 Rockstar bloggers are relationship builders.

#9 Rockstar bloggers are empirical.

#10 Rockstar bloggers constantly read, learn, test, and experiment.

How to Start Blogging. It might be easy to start a blog but sustaining it can be quite difficult. Running into writer's block, blogging for an audience of crickets, and attracting nasty commentators for the first time can take the wind out of your blogging sails. However, understand that every failure brings you closer to become a rockstar blogger.

Improving your blogging game requires you to have a deep desire for learning the ins and outs of successful blogging. But you have to play a long-term game. It is the hardest part because in the beginning nobody will care. So before you give up, try the strategies that follow.

It's a marathon, not a sprint. Develop an intense passion for your blogging exploits. What is passion? Close your eyes and think about what you would do if you could do anything. The first thing that comes to mind is your passion.

Constantly consume massive amounts of information related to your passion. Identify the best sources of information and be the first to know. Find people who accomplished success doing what you want to do and emulate them. For example, I look up to guys like Gary Vaynerchuk and Neil Patel.

Understanding the blogging game improves your skills pronto, so get serious about your approach at the outset.

Become a passion chaser. Follow your passion. Pick your niche based on an idea which makes your heart sing. Skilled, authority bloggers (aka rockstars) generally blog about ideas that appeal to them.

Think about the long, hard blogging road ahead. Some days you will not feel like posting. These are the days where following your passion comes in handy. Rockstar bloggers push themselves to create when writer's block seems overwhelming because they are passionate.

For Anna van Tonder of annaDishes.com, it was the passion for cooking that led her to build a food blog:

"Blogging has become so many things to me, so much more than just a food blog. It is an outlet, an inspiration, a collection, and meeting place. I started blogging at annaDishes for a few reasons. First, I'm a passionate foodie and love to share with and feed those around me. Second, whether it's food, ideas, or writing, I love to give what I can create for people—in person or virtually.

For starters, I think it is extremely important to have some true energy about a topic when looking to start a blog. I get excited to talk to people about food, recipes, parties, travel, big ideas and how to create. To really engage, you have to be passionate about your subject. If you don't believe in it, why should anyone else?"

Take successful baby steps. Successful bloggers create helpful content day after day. The best bloggers make strong connections daily.

Think in terms of months and years instead of hours and days when setting blogging goals. Build your blog on a solid foundation. Be patient. Relax.

Almost all failing bloggers allow impatience to cloud their judgment. Improve your blogging game by providing value and make connections by taking successful baby steps. Write one solid post today.

Meet 5 new bloggers. Follow these steps each day for 3 months, then 4 months, then 1 year. Each seemingly insignificant baby step can help you create a wildly successful blog.

Monetize after hitting the basics. No successful blogger chases money. Bump up your blogging IQ by learning the basics inside and out. It's only after you've created immense value that money will begin to flow into your coffers via blog monetization. Spending months making strong connections with fellow bloggers also boosts your net worth.

Frequency matters, but only if the content is good. The necessity of having a blog on your site is not really debatable. According to HubSpot, companies that blog receive 55 percent more website traffic, and B2C companies that blog receive 88 percent more leads than those that don't.

The topic of content frequency is my pet peeve, because it is often abused and taken to extremes, especially when it comes to blogging and branded content. It is either too frequent to retain a certain level of quality, or too infrequent to make any difference.

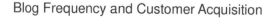

Blog Frequency and Customer Acquisition

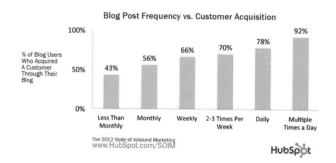

The above chart from Hubspot shows that customer acquisition and blog content go hand-in-hand. Content frequency does impact customer acquisition, but if the content is not good, your audience will move away and your efforts will be counter-productive.

Rockstar bloggers chase their passions, not dollars. Resist acting on the urge to get rich quick. Adopt a servant's mindset. Create value to gain your audience's trust. Make connections to grow your blogging network. Building something valuable helps you to attract value in the form of prospering relationships and money. Make money blogging only after you have mastered the basics.

Writing Magnetic Headlines

"Give me six hours to chop down a tree and I will spend the first four sharpening the axe." Abraham Lincoln

Many newbie (and sometimes even veteran) bloggers erroneously spend 95% of their time creating blog content and only 5% pondering headlines and titles. Unfortunately for these bloggers, most readers' attention spans expire in seconds.

Unless you reel in your readers instantly, your well-crafted content goes largely unnoticed and going viral becomes impossible.

Set aside at least 15 to 30 minutes for choosing a magnetic title after crafting your post.

List three to five intriguing titles guaranteed to increase your CTR and page views. After carefully thinking through each option, select the one that inspires you like no other. Ask your friends or followers for feedback.

Most importantly, test and learn from data you collect looking at engagement metrics such as social sharing and page views. Double down on best-performing headlines and keep testing new ways to engage your audience.

At my SearchDecoder.com blog we did an in-depth headline analysis looking at the most popular posts of 2013. The data included over 30K visits and 6K social shares. The results were originally published on Problogger.

Use power verbs. Use power verbs to goad readers into clicking on and sharing your content. Imagine yourself as a blogging commander, motivating swift action with assertiveness. Start titles with actionable verbs like "Read," "Download" or "Learn." Actionable verbs can be visualized and acted upon easily.

Keep things simple and never use a power verb in any spot other than the beginning of your title. Maximize the effectiveness of these action words.

Employ colorful adjectives. Colorful adjectives magnetically attract eager readers to your titles by appealing to the imagination. If readers can see in their minds-eye what you wish to convey, you will generate high CTR.

Pull out a thesaurus. Scour the manual to find descriptive, entertaining adjectives to lasso readers' eyeballs. Test words like 'awesome,' 'unstoppable,' and 'unconventional' to engage your reader's visualizing faculty.

By the way, the number-one most shared, read and commented on blog post on SearchDecoder is "10 Unconventional Keyword Research Tools to Include in Your SEO Toolbox." (Interestingly, the two blog posts I've published using the word 'unconventional' in the title made it to the top 10 most shared blog posts on SearchDecoder.com.)

Arouse curiosity. Reading provocative questions piques interest. Interested web visitors set the foundation for viral blog posts. Readers rarely scan question-themed titles without clicking through, because inquiring minds need to know.

Asking questions or exposing industry 'secrets' compels click-throughs because few can resist mystery. Observe the masterful novelist. Supreme writers craft cliffhangers filled with mystery and intrigue. How can anyone put down these page-turners when each chapter ends with either a question or another secret yet to be revealed?

One of the top shared blog posts on my blog, 'The 10 Secrets of Effective Bootstrap Digital Marketing for Startups.' leverages this tactic.

Build lists (always). Building list-themed headers is a surefire approach to crafting magnetic titles. In fact, 9 out of the 10 best performing posts on my blog included a list in the headline.

Testing various numbers in list headlines (I tested between 7 and 30) on my blog didn't indicate a clear winner (statistically), but the number 10 performed best.

Readers need gobs of information to satiate their curiosity. The average web cruiser craves thorough content. Sharing 11 tips or 8 steps to solve a particular problem draws readers in because they expect to find practical answers to their specific questions.

Jeff Goins notes how using obscure numbers in titles like 19 or 37 can appeal to readers. Experiment with different single and double-digit numbers to see which titles result in the most clicks.

The highest number in the list headline I used was 30 and it performed surprisingly well (contrary to the 'less is more' approach). The 30 Awesome Free SEO Tools for Small Businesses' headline was the 8th most popular blog post on Searchdecoder in 2013.

Use 'magic' words. "Quick," "Easy," and "Simple" are the magic headline words guaranteed to boost clicks pronto. Do you want to know the quick, easy or simple way to solve a problem you've been trying to address? Of course you do.

Appeal to today's Internet culture by using these magic words frequently. However, make sure that the solution is actually quick, easy or simple to keep your credibility intact.

Add "lessons" to your 'magic word' list. People read blogs to learn, and no matter how 'easy' your advice seems, it's always a good idea to anchor your findings in data, interviews, or case studies. The #5 best performer on SearchDecoder, "7 Lessons for Effective B2B Content Marketing via the Maersk Line Case Study," drew in eager students quickly.

Pick up the paper. Always learn from the pros. Read a newspaper or scour online news sites to find appealing blog post title ideas.

Follow the example of the "8 Internet Books You Should Read in 2014" post that performed exceptionally well for me during the slow Holiday period in December 2013. Whatever you are blogging about; there are tons of relevant books and blogs you can curate.

Mine the web or your local newsstand for creative, proven titles guaranteed to increase blog readership. Taking a cue from some of the best title writers on earth is a simple way to create a viral post.

Curating content proved to be the most low-effort, high-return activity on my blog. "The 8 Content Marketing Statistics You Need to Know" headline was the second best performer on SearchDecoder.com in 2013.

Headlines are visual. Did you know that 90% of communication is non-verbal? It's a social media world. If you want to increase the sharability and CTR of your blog posts, include eye-catching images and visuals and use them to populate your homepage and social media feed. Spend time choosing the best 'featured image' for every headlines.

Part 2: CODE

Congratulations – you've made it to Code, the second of our 5Cs. Fear not: you don't have to know any code, or want to learn any code, to apply the information in this chapter to improve your SEO and overall visibility on the web.

Still, you'll need to be familiar with a few technical terms because they're important to the way that search engines interact with the web pages and blog posts you'll be creating.

Ready? Here they are. Don't worry: we'll explain fully and simply what each one of these terms means later on.

Page Title tags. Just as a headline defines what an article is about, the Page Title tag describes what the web page is about to search engines.

Meta description tags describe your site or page to search engines in more detail. They're important, but far less important than Title tags.

Alt tags are used to describe the contents of images to search engines (which can't interpret the meaning of images without some help).

URL Structure. URL structure pertains to the way pages appear on your site (for example, mysite.com/mypage.html). It's important to search engines (and we'll show you how to get it right)

Schema.org Markup. Think of schema.org markup as another way you can give search engines a way to understand your content better.

Okay... I know what you're thinking: this stuff is dry! But please don't succumb to the temptation to skip ahead past this chapter. Stick with it because it's important (and the terms that are discussed will pop up in later chapters, which we promise will be more fun than this one).

Seeing the Web Through the Eyes of Google

Why are tags, URL structure and Schema.org important to know about? Because search engines – although they incorporate billions of dollars worth of human and machine intelligence – are like people who lack the ability to hear, see, or sense anything that's not presented to them in a code they can interpret.

Someday search engines might become intelligent enough to instantly know the meaning of every piece of content they encounter. But right now, if you want to communicate with a search engine, you've got to use "code."

SEO-Browser.com is a tool that allows you to see your website as search engines see it.

How Search Engines Work

Ready for some more technical jargon? We'll keep it to a minimum. But we'll need a bit of it to understand how search engines do their magic. Welcome to the wonderful world of bots, indexes and queries.

Bots. Bots (abbreviated from "robots" and also known as "crawlers") are small programs that search engines send out across the Web to gather information about the sites and pages on it. Bots aren't very smart – they can't understand anything – but like good clerks, they record everything they encounter. And they also have no free will: they can only follow links from one site to another.

Indexes. Bots are programmed to report back to the search engine that sent them. Once a bot reports back, the data it's gathered is copied to the Index, a massive database.

Queries. Queries are strings of text typed in by users of search engines to answer questions. If certain words (keywords) match terms that are in the Index, the sites which the bot has reported are using these words will appear on the search engine's results page.

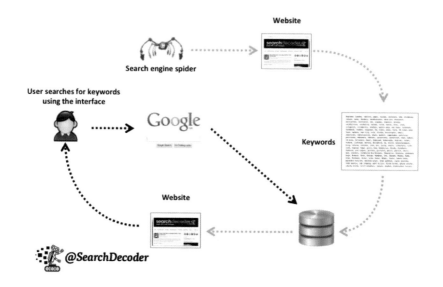

To summarize:

Bots **crawl** websites in order to discover content to add to a search engine's index.

Bots **find** new content add it to the search engines from links within other pieces of content.

Bots **index** content trying to learn what the content is about.

When people search for specific keywords, search engines **serve up the content** that will most likely fulfill the searcher's needs. The content served up ranks in order of popularity and authority, both of which are determined by ranking factors such as links and social shares.

So how is all of this relevant to your job – improving the SEO performance of your site?

The links you build to pages on your website help bots discover them.

The keywords you use to optimize those pages help indexes categorize them.

The links and social shares your pages receive help the search engine determine the page's popularity.

Let's look at how you can apply SEO strategies to get your content discovered by search engines and delivered to your target audience!

Mining Golden Nugget Keywords

What are Golden Nugget Keywords? Words and phrases, typed into a search engine by users, that will deliver desirable visitors to your site.

Competition for generic keywords is fierce. For example, every pizzeria in Brooklyn will want their results to appear when a user types in the keyword phrase, "best pizza in Brooklyn."

Golden Nugget Keywords are different. They're just as valuable in terms of driving traffic that will result in business, but fewer people are competing for them. That's why it's crucial that you discover them.

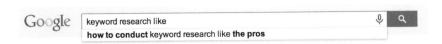

I always start my keyword research with the Google's search bar. As you start typing your keyword, Google will complete the query for you, featuring the most popular search terms.

To find your own Golden Nugget Keywords, answer the following questions:

What keywords are your customers likely to use to find you?

You likely know the keywords that your customers will use when trying to find your website. These keywords may have been used on the phone, in an email, or when talking to you or your employees in person.

People might have referenced those keywords when talking about your business, or similar businesses they have dealt with in the past by saying things like, "The last home builder I worked with didn't give us the option to customize our floor plan." or "We are in the market for a custom home builder." Between these two references, you know that 'home builder' and 'custom home' 'builder' are two apt keywords to describe your business.

The same can holds for the individual products and services your business offers. When people call your business, what do they ask for? If you receive many calls asking for a quote on kitchen remodeling, then you know that 'kitchen remodeling' is an accurate keyword phrase for that particular service.

Brainstorm keywords for your website by creating a list of keywords that customers use to reference your business, your products, and your services. Link each keyword with a particular page on your website. For example, if the keyword describes your business as a whole, it may appear on your homepage. If it describes a particular product or service, post the keyword on your product or service landing page.

What keywords are your competitors using?

If you're having trouble coming up with keywords from your customers, check out your competitors' keywords. Type their names into Google. The text linked to their websites (also known as their Page Title tags - remember that one?) will have the top keyword phrases that they are targeting.

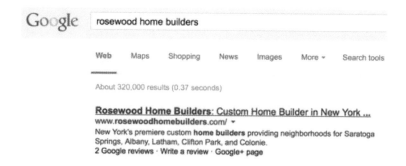

In this example you can see both 'home builders' and 'custom home builder'. Click through to the website and click on the main product and service pages. At the top of your browser window or tab, you'll see the SEO title for those individual pages, which should include more keywords.

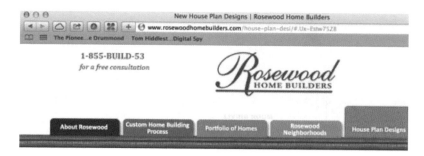

At the top of this browser window, you can see 'house plan designs.' You should see the same as you click through to other key areas of your competitor's website.

Take some time to jot down keywords that your competitors use on their homepages and on pages for their top products and services.

Do these keywords attract buyers or content consumers?

Analyze each keyword for commercial intent. Would someone search for the keyword because he or she is looking to make a purchase or would someone search for the keyword because he or she is looking for more information?

Google can usually answer this question for you quickly. Search for the keywords on your list. If the results include businesses offering a product or service, it's a keyword that people use when they intend to buy. If the results include Wikipedia results, blogs, and articles, then it's likely a keyword that people use when they intend to learn more about a topic. It's the difference between searches for "home builders" and "building a home." The first shows likely commercial intent; the second doesn't.

Just because you discern a keyword is used more for informational purposes than buying purposes doesn't mean it needs to be scrapped. It just means you need to use it differently. Instead of using 'building a home' on your homepage, use it in a blog post. This way, you can connect with people who are searching for information and provide them enough information to ultimately land them as a customer at a later point in time.

Do your keywords get enough searches?

Here's where tools come in. The last thing you will want to do with the keyword list you've developed is find out how many people search for it. The **Google AdWords Keyword Planner** can show you an estimated number of searches for each keyword you enter.

Search terms		Avg. monthly searches ?	Competition ?	Suggested bid ?	Ad impr. share ?	Add to plan
home builders	⊵	9,900	High	$2.96	0%	»
custom home builders	⊵	4,400	High	$3.37	0%	»
home builder	⊵	1,900	High	$4.14	0%	»
luxury home builders	⊵	1,000	High	$2.99	0%	»
custom home builder	⊵	1,000	High	$3.11	0%	»
luxury home builder	⊵	210	High	$2.75	0%	»

In addition to getting the search volume for your keywords, you'll get additional keyword suggestions.

Keyword (by relevance)		Avg. monthly searches ?	Competition ?	Suggested bid ?	Ad impr. share ?	Add to plan
home	⊵	368,000	Low	$2.95	0%	»
home plans	⊵	40,500	High	$0.53	0%	»
home design	⊵	18,100	High	$1.66	0%	»
modular home prices	⊵	9,900	High	$1.06	0%	»
home floor plans	⊵	8,100	Medium	$0.51	0%	»
log home plans	⊵	6,600	High	$0.80	0%	»
dream home	⊵	6,600	Low	$0.60	0%	»
home remodeling	⊵	5,400	High	$6.10	0%	»
modular home	⊵	5,400	High	$1.14	0%	»
luxury home plans	⊵	4,400	High	$0.63	0%	»
design your own home	⊵	4,400	Medium	$1.10	0%	»

The key with this tool is to not focus on the exact numbers. You won't be guaranteed to get 4,400 visitors each month if you rank #1 for 'custom home builders.' These are just estimated average monthly searches. Determine which keywords have the most searches. If you can't decide between two keywords, eliminate one based on the number of searches.

The suggested keyword ideas can help you discover new keywords to use on your internal pages.

Keyword Research Toolbox

Here are a couple of tried-and-proven keyword research tools you may consider adding to your arsenal.

Google's Keyword Planner. Allows you to locate keywords based on your actual search queries and volume. Use for keyword research and discovery.

Google Trends. Formerly Insights for Search. Shows you what is trending online and what people are searching for. Use for identifying trending keywords.

Keyword Eye. Keyword Eye is a suite of affordable, fast, no-nonsense visual keyword and competitor research tools to help with your PPC and SEO campaigns.

Keyword Discovery. Provides you with insights and ideas for keywords that helps you to improve SEO content, PPC campaign growth and performance.

Ubersuggest. Get keyword ideas with Übersuggest, the free keyword suggestion tool that makes good use of Google Suggest and other suggest services.

SEMRush. Provides you with insights on how competing sites are performing in search. Use to check how competitors are ranking on keywords.

Soovle. This tool was suggested by our community in the comments section of a blog post about keyword research tools. I tested it and I think it provides a nice visual way of aggregating keyword data from Google, Amazon, Bing, and Yahoo.

Answers.com. Helpful to identify niches and long-tail keywords.

Now that you know how to find the right keywords, let's learn how to optimize your website with your newfound keywords.

You'll learn how to do this in the next section. But first, remember that list of dry terms we mentioned earlier (SEO Title Tags, URL Structure, Schema, etc.)? You'll be hearing from them again in the next section. Why? Because they play leading roles in the drama of plugging your Golden Nugget keywords into your site so that they draw valuable traffic to it.

Optimizing Your Site

Site optimization starts with a self-evaluation. You need to look at your website with a critical eye to identify areas for improvement. This process is known as a website audit.

"Website audits serve the same purpose as a physical. They're an opportunity to take a complete, top-to-bottom accounting of a site to note what is working, what's broken, and what needs to be improved. Once completed, the audit should help inform the larger strategy and sometimes, shape the desired outcomes and the time frame in which those goals will be reached."

Explains Jason White, Director of SEO and Technical SEO Whiz at DragonSearch.

You need to look at a website from the perspective of a user, which search engines are essentially trying to do. Users are savvy; they have an abundance of choices and they know they don't have to deal with a company that isn't focused on their needs, so we start by looking at the site from their perspective.

Here are a couple of questions that we ask ourselves when we audit a website:

Does the site serve a need, does it answer a problem, and can a visitor come to the homepage and know instantly what products and services are offered?

Are the resources well thought out, are blog posts simply written because it's a best practice, or are they focused and high quality?

What happens when a user fills out a form, picks up the phone, or makes a purchase?

An SEO audit is a collaborative project. Part of constantly hunting for improvements requires your SEO team to run the project with efficiency in mind so we can dig to find every last issue and detail that makes a site unique. We want this mindset to ooze over to both the client's internal team and the development team to earn buy-in so we can get tasks completed quickly.

SEO Audit Tools

Screaming Frog. Allows you to quickly analyze, audit, and review a site from an onsite SEO perspective. It fetches key onsite page elements for SEO, presents them in tabs by type, and allows you to filter for common SEO issues, or slice and dice the data how you see fit by exporting into Excel.

Ad Planner. A media planning/research tool that uses inputs about users' target audience and key demographic to provide information about the websites they likely visit.

WayBack Machine. Created by the Internet Archive, provides users with archived versions of websites called, 'three dimensional index.'

Alexa. Uses global web metrics to allow users to find the most successful websites based on category, country, or keyword and allows users to optimize their web presence. Check your score at Alexa.com.

The Only On-Site SEO Tool You'll Ever Need

Install **Yoast** at the outset when you create your WordPress blog. It will help you install the key SEO metadata and optimizations without any technical or coding skills. This plugin is written by Joost de Valk and his team at Yoast to improve your site's SEO on all needed aspects.

Although this WordPress SEO plugin goes the extra mile to take care of all the technical optimization, it first and foremost helps you write better content. WordPress SEO forces you to choose a focus keyword when you're writing your articles, and then makes sure you use that focus keyword everywhere.

If you are not using WordPress, you will need to access the HTML and insert certain pieces of code. I included both methods in this book.

The following are the most important elements of your website's on-site optimization. Each tip is a Google-friendly technique to help boost your rankings. Add these elements to your homepage, product pages, and your content pages such as your blog and FAQ.

Page Title Tag

The Page Title tag is the title of a page on your website. Include your primary keyword – and secondary if applicable – within this title tag. The structure for your SEO title tag generally looks like this in your webpage's HTML code:

```
                    <head>
   <title>Keyword Phrase 1 and Keyword Phrase 2 – Company
                    Name</title>
                    </head>
```

The Page Title tag is the text used to link to your website in search results. Make sure the title accurately describes your website and is clickable to boost traffic.

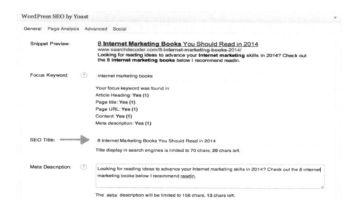

Meta Description Tag

The Meta description tag is the description for your document (up to 160 characters), or in this case, a page on your website. The Meta description doesn't help you rank for particular keywords, but is seen in search results as the 'snippet' (a short section of text) that appears beneath your link.

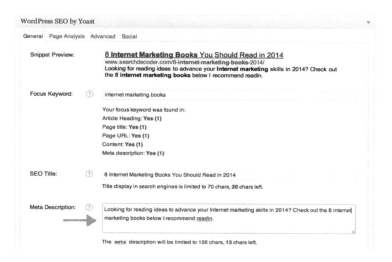

Improperly written Meta descriptions can discourage people to click through to your website. Good ones will attract them. The structure for your meta description tag looks like this in your webpage's HTML code:

```
<head>
<title>Keyword Phrase 1 and Keyword Phrase 2 - Company
Name</title>
<meta name="description" content="Here is a description of
Company Name that offers Keyword Phrase 1 and Keyword
Phrase 2.">
</head>
```

Alt Tag

Alt tags are text descriptions of each image used on a webpage. Remember, search engines can't determine what any image on your site means without some help from you. Alt tags helped them do this, and they help you optimize your image for specific keywords. The structure for Alt tags generally looks like this in your webpage's HTML code:

```
<img src="http://www.yourdomain.com/images/keyword-
phrase.png" alt="Keyword Phrase" />
```

Use your keywords in both the filename and the Alt tag of the image. This helps search engine bots determine what the page linked to your image is about and increases the likelihood that your image will do well in Google Image search.

URL Structure

Including keywords in your URL is another good way to help optimize each web page for a particular keyword. So instead of this:

http://www.yourdomain.com/p?=123

You want to set up a URL structure that looks like this:

http://www.yourdomain.com/keyword-phrase-for-page/

Properly optimized URLs help bots and people determine what your webpage is about.

8 Internet Marketing Books You Should Read in 2014

Permalink: http://www.searchdecoder.com/ 8-internet-marketing-books-2014 / OK Cancel Get Shortlink

Okay – now you know why all of this is important. Now you probably want to know "how the heck do I do all of this?" Don't worry: it's a lot easier than it you think.

You don't have to hire a coder or a developer to get any of this done. In fact, it's amazingly easy to accomplish all of this, if you use the right publishing platform for your site (I recommend Wordpress), and choose the right SEO plug-in (I like Yoast).

Before we get to that, we need to introduce another oddly-named entity that's shaken up the SEO world called Hummingbird.

Why? Because knowing about it will help you create the best, most search-attractive pages you can possibly make. And that's the whole purpose: to make sure you market like it's 2014.

Feeding the Hummingbird

Introducing Hummingbird is Stephen C. Baldwin, Editor-in-Chief at Didit.com, a company I consulted with at the time of publishing this book. He's both a birdwatcher (who runs the popular BrooklynParrots.com site) and a content strategist who knows a thing or two about creating search-worthy Web content.

In September 2013, Google announced that it had updated a core algorithm influencing the way that the results of complex queries appear on the Google SERP. This update was called 'Hummingbird' and was designed to better handle the type of 'question/answer' – style queries prevalent on mobile devices. Google has stated that Hummingbird applies to up to 90 percent of search queries, making its effects nearly universal.

How Does Hummingbird Work?

Google has released no formal documentation on Hummingbird, a situation that has led to a high level of conjecture and misinformation about it to circulate within the SEO community. What's beyond doubt is that Hummingbird uses a lot of different sources to determine how important any given web page or site is.

These sources include a synonym engine, the Knowledge Graph, the search history of users, document meta-information, geo-location data, and other sources associated with the searcher's known identity to better establish the search intent of 'verbose' queries. These inputs augment (but do not replace) all of the factors in prior use by Google to establish site and page authority.

What Should you Do?

It's clear that web publishers need to think more holistically about the content they generate and optimize in order to increase the chances that it will rank favorably on the Google SERP. Additionally, they may need to take steps to identify themselves better to Google to gain the search engine's trust, and organize the data on their sites in a way that is easy for Google to understand.

You should do three things to make Hummingbird happy (which will make searchers happy as well):

Optimize content naturally. Hummingbird should cause

copywriters to focus on themes — not just keywords — when crafting content. While keywords remain important, the fact that Hummingbird is better able to understand the *context* of a particular body of text means that writers can write more naturally, without obsessing about keyword density (how many times a keyword shows up in a body of text).

If content is written naturally, with a goal in mind and a structure leading the reader to that goal, Hummingbird should be fully able to understand what's being written and why it should be relevant to a particular searcher operating in the particular context in which the query is made (mobile, research, or commercial query context).

Disclose your identity to Google. While Google has denied that social signals are incorporated into search rankings, it is clear that the more Google knows about a given publisher, the more likely it is that such a publisher (if legitimate) will be correctly accorded the credit he/she is due. At minimum, publishers seeking to take advantage of Hummingbird should have Google Accounts in order to verify their identities.

These accounts provide both utility (Gmail) and a range of tools (Google Analytics, Webmaster Tools) that provide major intelligence value to the publisher when it comes to site optimization and content strategy. While having an active Google account is not tantamount to having an official "seal of approval" from Google, it demonstrates that one has "nothing to hide," a quality that Google (which is continually battling information pollution from anonymous or quasi-anonymous spammers) takes very seriously. Additionally, publishers should take steps to incorporate Author Rel to correctly assign authorship to web documents.

Structure your data. Structuring web documents correctly will enhance Hummingbird's ability to understand and correctly contextualize web content. While HTML — the native language of the Web — has some logical structure already built into it (H1, H2, etc.), publishers should take steps to more granularly tag their documents by applying micro-data format tagging as specified by schema.org.

Using Schema For Non-Techies

Schema is a big subject - in fact it's so big that we really couldn't publish this book in good conscience without including a discussion from Brady Callahan, a Schema expert.

Fear not; Brady does a great job of making all of this geeky terminology (itemscope, itemtype, etc.) as accessible as possible.

Stick with us, because the results will pay off for you big time! However, if you just starting out and doesn't feel the insights below are actionable for you at this time, come back to this section later when you are ready.

Schema Optimization Basics

What is Schema? Schema is the preferred markup search engines — Google, Bing, and others — recommend webmasters use to 'mark-up' their website's HTML pages. Its purpose is to increase the major search providers' understanding of the web in order to create better, more in-depth search results.

The search engines rely on this microdata to improve and diversify search results, helping users more easily find the best webpages for respective search queries. Google wants users to find the best answers as quickly as possible, and schema helps them sort and rank web content more efficiently.

In short, websites that implement schema markup help search engines help users by serving higher-quality search results.

Microdata from schema.org is important because of the heavy impact it has on search engine results pages (SERPs). When you mark up certain content on your website with schema, you're helping the search engines understand 'exactly' what your content is and how it should be treated.

For example, when a search engine bot crawls your site and finds a page about 'the Iron Horse,' how does it know if you're referring to the band, the 1924 silent film, or the bicycle company?

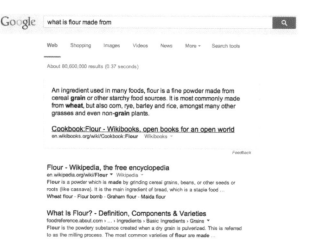

Schema data helps search engines categorize the different 'iron horses' into entities they can grasp and understand, creating a more relevant SERP that better serves users.

Gravity (2013) - IMDb

www.imdb.com/title/tt1454468/ ▾ Internet Movie Database ▾

★★★★★ Rating: 8/10 - 400,468 votes

Gravity -- Astronauts Ryan Stone and Matt Kowalski are on a routine ... Sandra Bullock at event of Gravity (2013) Still of Sandra Bullock in Gravity (2013) Emma ...

Awards - Trivia - Gravity Reviews & Ratings - Full Cast & Crew

This creates unique 'snippets' — additional content under or along with the main listing — in the SERPs that stand out in a dramatic way. There's even data that shows these snippets attract more attention and clicks from users than links that do not include them.

Best Hot Dogs Recipe : Michael Chiarello : Food Network

www.foodnetwork.com/.../best-hot-dogs-reci... ▾ Food Network ▾

★★★★★ Rating: 4 - 7 reviews - 12 mins

For an added kick of flavor try splitting the boiled dogs almost all the way in half. Open them up and add to a hot pan which a little olive oil has been added. Cook ...

One of the most obvious examples of the importance of using Schema is the Google Knowledge Graph, a SERP feature that is fed by a complicated link graph that understands entities and the relationships among them.

Thomas Jefferson

3rd U.S. President

Thomas Jefferson was an American Founding Father, the principal author of the Declaration of Independence and the third President of the United States. Wikipedia

Born: April 13, 1743, Shadwell, VA

Died: July 4, 1826, Charlottesville, VA

Education: College of William and Mary (1760–1762)

Presidential term: March 4, 1801 – March 4, 1809

Awards: AIA Gold Medal

Children: Martha Jefferson Randolph, Mary Jefferson Eppes, Lucy Elizabeth Jefferson, Jane Jefferson, Peter Jefferson

People also search for   View 15+ more

John Adams   George Washington   Benjamin Franklin   James Madison   Alexander Hamilton

Using schema markup enables your web pages to appear with a variety of different snippets, helping them stand out from the rest of the results, receive more clicks, hopefully leading to additional business.

Do you care about increasing traffic to your website, expanding your customer base, and growing your business' online revenue?

Then you should care about schema.

How Do I Add Schema to My Website? Like other microdata formats, schema is added directly into the HTML code, providing search engines with additional context when they crawl a web page. Schema.org provides a real-life example by using the 2009 blockbuster hit movie, "Avatar."

```
<div>
  <h1>Avatar</h1>
  <span>Director: James Cameron (born August 16, 1954)</span>
  <span>Science fiction</span>
  <a href="../movies/avatar-theatrical-trailer.html">Trailer</a>
</div>
```

The following screenshots of HTML show a basic comparison of a snippet of plain-HTML code versus a snippet that's full of schema markup to help search engines understand exactly what "Avatar" is, who is involved in the project, and the genre of film.

This is done using three of the most common elements of schema:

item **scope**, item **type**, and item **prop**.

While these terms may currently have no meaning to you, they're quite simple for beginners to grasp. They represent the hierarchy by which all schema data is incorporated into HTML on a webpage.

```
<div itemscope>
  <h1>Avatar</h1>
  <span>Director: James Cameron (born August 16, 1954) </span>
  <span>Science fiction</span>
  <a href="../movies/avatar-theatrical-trailer.html">Trailer</a>
</div>
```

By adding the itemscope element, you're notifying the search engine that the following block of information is about a particular item. You're defining the item's scope, if you will.

```
<div itemscope itemtype="http://schema.org/Movie">
  <h1>Avatar</h1>
  <span>Director: James Cameron (born August 16, 1954)</span>
  <span>Science fiction</span>
  <a href="../movies/avatar-theatrical-trailer.html">Trailer</a>
</div>
```

Second, within the itemscope element is the item type, allowing you to tell the search engine what type of item the following block of information is. In this example, 'Avatar' is correctly categorized under the movie type.

```
<div itemscope itemtype="http://schema.org/Movie">
  <h1>Avatar</h1>
  <span>Director: James Cameron (born August 16, 1954)</span>
  <span>Science fiction</span>
  <a href="../movies/avatar-theatrical-trailer.html">Trailer</a>
</div>
```

Finally, itemprop allows you to drill deeper into a particular itemtype, providing details on other people, places, and things related to the respective item.

```
<div itemscope itemtype ="http://schema.org/Movie">
  <h1 itemprop="name">Avatar</h1>
  <span>Director: <span itemprop="director">James Cameron</span> (born August 16, 1954)</span>
  <span itemprop="genre">Science fiction</span>
  <a href="../movies/avatar-theatrical-trailer.html" itemprop="trailer">Trailer</a>
</div>
```

At the end of the example, the search engine not only understands that "Avatar" is a movie, but it knows that James Cameron directed the film, and it understands that it falls under the science fiction genre.

These details will go a long way to help Google and other search engines return a better result for the search queries relevant to this page. The information may even be included in the Knowledge Graph or in an answer box, a "pop out" result at the top of the SERP that gets a significant amount of a SERP's impressions and clicks.

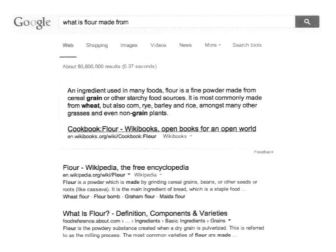

'Movie' is one of thousands of itemtypes — and their corresponding itemprops — you have at your disposal. Your business, regardless of the industry or niche it's in, or the content you create, has an opportunity to use schema markup.

The Future of Schema, Machine Learning, and Snippets

The schema vocabulary will only continue to grow. Search engine understanding — we're essentially talking about machine learning here — is an endless endeavor that will never be 'complete.' The number of itemtypes and itemprops will expand and multiply in the name of further understanding of entities and the relationships among them.

Schema markup can produce snippets for a variety of content — recipes, videos, reviews, and more — but Google is also always tweaking their SERPs, adding and removing snippets as their algorithm sees fit.

However, I maintain the biggest benefit to adding schema to your website now is to be ahead of the curve. As of the summer of 2014, according to Searchmetrics, **less than 1% of U.S. domains have schema markup implemented**.

Whether you're an owner of a business big or small, an experienced webmaster, or a novice SEO, it's time to join the effort to build a smarter web!

Part 3: CREDIBILITY

LINK BUILDING

+ AUTHOR POPULARITY

What is credibility? The quality of being believed or trusted.

On the Internet, credibility is a big problem because people can cloak their identities very easily. Credibility is something that you have to earn by providing content that's useful and trustworthy, If you do this, you will naturally acquire links to your site and pages that Google will interpret as 'votes in your favor.'

But credibility isn't something you can buy. Like your own reputation, it's something that may take you a long time to build up. And like reputation, it's something that can be destroyed in a moment, if, that is, you succumb to the temptation of trying to 'fake it.'

In this section, we'll show you how search engines measure

credibility, and how you can build up your own credibility by accumulating natural, editorial links — the ones that search engines like best, and by showing search engines that the people who create you content — your authors — have credibility themselves.

Credibility = High-Quality Links to Your Site

Off-site search engine optimization, aka the 'infamous' link building, gets a bad rap for being difficult. In truth, if you have valuable content and build strong relationships, credible people will want to link to you.

There are tons of tricks, tips, tools, and techniques that you can discover by researching the link building process. Those will be the tactics in your toolbox, as long they are ethical.

However, attracting quality backlinks to your website is no small task. The foundation of building your online credibility lies in your ability to create amazing content and build social connections.

Build your credibility beyond the Internet. Engage in public speaking, by attending industry events, and by guest blogging. If you can make a serious impact where you pop up and your audience finds value in your content, you gain the trust of your target audience. This trust will lead you to build your online credibility, because if people actually know you in the "real world," they're far more likely to link to you online.

Focus on quality over quantity. Don't publish five mediocre, off the top of my head articles, a week on five mediocre websites. Publish one great, well-researched article instead so that your content is actually worth a link. Don't fall for inexpensive packages or services from sketchy vendors that guarantee your website will be #1 in search results without telling you how they intend to achieve that goal.

Establish credibility with patience in mind. Don't force the trust-building process. Persistently build bonds with authorities in your niche to slowly and steadily gain trust and to optimize your SEO campaign.

Interview pros working in your industry, set up Google Authorship to establish your authority in search engines, and use social media to augment your outreach campaign. Developing strong bonds with serious authorities in your niche can greatly enhance your credibility.

Stay away from black hat link building. Doing this can utterly destroy your hard-earned credibility. A good rule of thumb to tell if it's black hat is when link building is sold to you for a couple of hundred bucks, or when the package includes items such as directory submissions, commenting, guest blog posting on low-quality sites, and multiple press releases (sounds familiar?). Those tactics are not sustainable and will eventually get you in trouble with Google.

"The objective of link building is that it is natural, and not that it appears to be natural."

Matt Cutts, Head of Webspam at Google

Measuring Your Credibility

In your own life, you probably have a pretty good idea about who can be trusted and who can't, and who you should listen to (and who you shouldn't). On the Internet, there are a bunch of useful metrics that can serve as proxies for the traditional information about people and firms that's passed "through the grapevine."

PageRank

PageRank is a way of thinking about the importance of any given web page by looking at all of the web pages that link to it, while also factoring in the importance of the linking pages.

In Google's words, "PageRank works by counting the number and quality of links to a page to determine a rough estimate of how important the website is. The underlying assumption is that more important websites are likely to receive more links from other websites."

PageRank is presented on the 0-10 scale; the higher your score the better.

Use tools such as **CheckPageRank.net** or **PRChecker.net** to check PageRank of any domain. You can also install the **SEOQuake** browser plugin to instantly check the strength of a domain or a web page.

Domain/Page Authority

Domain/Page Authority isn't an official metric used by Google or Bing. It was developed by a 3rd party (Moz.com, a search research firm) that attempts to approximate the relative importance of any site. Domain Authority uses a 100-point scale to score this importance.

It's a very useful tool for webmasters to use to see how their sites stack up against competitors.

Use Moz's **Open Site Explorer** tool to view the domain authority of any web site on the Web. You can do multiple competitor comparison. I also find the **MozBar**, a browser plug-in, very useful because it allows me to check the competitive SEO environment for ranking opportunity when I search Google.

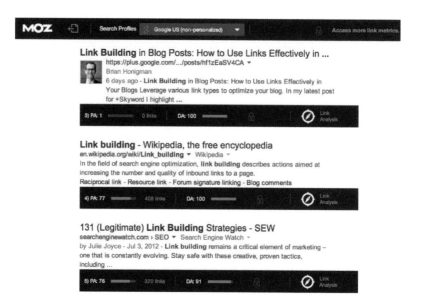

Author Rank

Just as web sites and pages have credibility (or not), so do the authors and content creators who produce them. Author Rank is a way of knowing about whether a given content creator has a track record of excellence on the Internet, or whether he/she (or it, because sometimes robots create content) hasn't earned such respect.

Author authority is synonymous with the 'ClearVoice Score,' a measure of an online author's complete body of digitally published work and its social relevance. We measure authority based on these metrics:

— The domain authority of the published content
— The power of the site the writer published their content on
— The frequency of the articles published by the writer
— The quantity of articles published by the writer
— The variety of domains the writer publishes to
— The social relevance of each individual piece of content

The score also takes into account a publishers' authorship semantics, which determines proper credit for content created.

"There's a large quantity of writers on the web today, but quantity is not what is important. What is important is the quality of the writer, and the quality of work that is produced. Google can now easily filter out thin, content farm/ghost-written content and each day they seem to more and more reward the content (and content creators) that has value to long-tail, semantic searches." Explains Allie Gray Freeland, PR Director at iAcquire.

ClearView is a new free tool that attempts to measure author rank and I like it.

ClearVoice co-founders Joe Griffin and Jay Swansson saw a need for creating an objective measure of content creators. They thought: "Wouldn't it be cool if we could somehow rank authors, journalists, and bloggers on the power of their voices based on the principles of authorship?"

They answered by creating a powerful, empirical author score. What ClearVoice does is gives businesses a transparent look into subject matter expert writers within their industry while simultaneously giving writers the ability to share their work and create real economic value for themselves.

If you are blogger, you can check your author rank by searching for your own name. Benchmark it and work to improve it by publishing on high-value blogs.

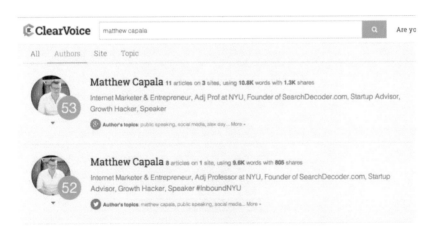

Tools such as ClearVoice have a huge benefit not only for writers, but also PR professionals and SEO link builders.

Earning High-Quality Backlinks

Search engines use backlinks (links from other sites to yours) to determine how important your own site is. Because they're such an important factor in assigning credibility, much of traditional SEO has been concerned with acquiring them (often through black hat techniques).

Search engines take any attempt to 'game' the system by paying for links or participating in link exchange schemes very seriously, because it subverts their quest to provide the best content to users. The result can be a penalty that can put you out of business.

Backlinks – real ones – have to be earned. This means a lot of hard work, patience, and persistence. But you can leap ahead of the pack if you learn the skills required for earning such backlinks, which is why we're glad that Brian Dean, link building mastermind and founder of Backlinko, contributed this very helpful article on the topic.

What skills are involved in effective link building?

Empathy: When you put yourself in someone else's shoes you're forced to answer the question:

Why should someone link to me? Do they like sharing controversial content? Or do they prefer how-to guides? Are they generous linkers or do they need some warming up before your pitch?

Empathy also helps you send killer outreach emails. When you understand the other person, you write in a voice that resonates with them.

Better outreach emails=more links.

Sales: Empathy is great, but the best link builders are closers. Like any good salesperson, you need to push buttons that get people to ACT. Otherwise, you're not going to convince them to take time out of their busy schedule to log into WordPress and add your link.

Content Marketing and Writing: Link building without great content is like bringing a knife to a gunfight. The person you're reaching out to will ultimately link to you based on the merit of the content on your site (also, outstanding content has a better chance of generating natural links).

Web Design and UX: Like anything in business, your content's presentation is massively important. Amazing copy and value hidden behind an ugly, Geocities-style site design can put a roadblock between you and some quality links.

Imagine how differently you would react to these two pages about SEO. Here's the first one

(http://www.vaughns-1-pagers.com/internet/seo-optimization.htm)

Okay — how about this one:

(http://www.quicksprout.com/the-advanced-guide-to-seo/)

You probably didn't need to read a single word to prefer the QuickSprout page, right?

Well it's the same story with the people you ask to link to you. A really, really nicely designed page can double or triple the links that you build to that piece of content.

How has the link building game evolved?

It's funny: I'd say link building is back to where it was 10 years ago before we had industrial-level link spam.

Back then, the best link building advice at the time was: Build an awesome site and tell other site owners about it with email outreach. From 2005-2012 or so, that advice didn't ring true because spam worked better. So link building devolved for a while. Google's Penguin algorithm update changed all that. Today, link building is back to where it all started: creating great resources and promoting them with email outreach.

Create and promote amazing resources. There's no shortcut here: this takes a ton of work. But the ROI on an amazing piece that solves your target audience's problems is insane... especially compared to paid traffic.

Guest posting. No, it's not dead. As long as you don't go overboard and build links from irrelevant sites, you'll be fine. And if guest post links do stop passing SEO value, they'll still send you traffic. In fact, Buffer built their entire business on a great product + guest posting=$$$ model.

Business listing pages. You'd be surprised by how many authoritative pages online simply list (and link to) businesses. For example, let's say that you have a startup in New York. You can easily get a link from a PageRank 7 page: "How do you get that link?" Fill out a simple form. Done. Also try searching for things like lists of travel apps or fitness startups to find pages that cater to your startup's industry. Reach out to them.

Create, speak, and sponsor events. One of the best things about the startup community is how they love to meet in real life. When you become involved in events, you'll generate links. And if you want a guaranteed link, just speak or sponsor an event – organizers always link to speakers and sponsors!

Partnerships. Bootstrap entrepreneurs do business formally or informally with other businesses. But they usually don't ask them to get a link from the people they work with. Huge opportunity for easy (and white hat) links.

Digital PR = Link Building 2.0

I have been an outspoken advocate of digital PR, which essentially is a form of outreach using digital technologies. Last year, Adotos.com quoted me saying:

"In a world where bloggers are journalists and consumers look for news on Google and YouTube, SEO and PR teams need to be like husband and wife: synched up and synergized. Traditional link building is dead and needs to be replaced by innovative content promotion strategies, centered around PR outreach and leveraging an existing brand's relationships. For enterprise-level brands, digital PR is link building 2.0, but only if SEO is involved. Together, SEO and PR have become the core business channels."

The benefits of PR on your online visibility are obvious, so a sound SEO strategy needs to leverage smart PR strategies: not those of placing links in press releases and submitting them across multiple directories, but those of telling captivating stories and building relationships with influencers and gatekeepers through digital media,

The Importance of Actively Managing Your PR

The importance of managing PR is becoming increasingly evident in the startup world. Unfortunately, there are still many startups who don't think they "need" PR. The problem is that public relations isn't a choice. Any entity, be it an individual or a business, has an involuntary relationship with the public. That relationship will continue to exist regardless of whether it's acknowledged or managed. Choosing not to focus any energy on building it is a mistake. In the on-demand, connected world we live in, the belief that PR should take a backseat can be fatal for startups.

Says Joseph McKeating Founder of Pulsar Strategy and Editor at Editorial IV, in a recent installment of Q&A with SearchDecoder.

Joe began his career working as a publicist for consumer brands at Rubenstein PR in midtown Manhattan before moving on to Prosek Partners. Realizing the value that good storytelling, proper messaging, and PR can add to startups, and convinced that big agency life was not for him, Joseph founded Pulsar Strategy, a small and nimble startup PR firm.

What are the PR myths? One of the biggest myths is that in order to succeed you need to work with a "PR guru." General rule of thumb: be skeptical of those who refer to themselves as gurus. The best people I've ever dealt with in public relations are not geniuses – they're scrappy, calculated and energetic. That's what it takes to succeed. Effort and strategy trump all other characteristics.

Another myth is that people in public relations are either (a) unintelligent or (b) shady. Compared to other industries, there is a low barrier to entry. This is a problem that industry gatekeepers have brought upon us and that several people – myself included – are working to change. Don't be fooled though, there are plenty of people in PR who would have excelled in any field. As far as being shady, this belief is based on the notion that public relations is the work of 'spin doctors.' You can find cases to support that belief, but public relations as a whole has moved way beyond that.

How to measure your Digital PR success? Thanks to technology and digital media, we're more capable than ever of measuring public relations efforts. Let's start with some of the historical issues, then move on to solutions available today.

There are still some intangibles. For example, building a brand that is engaging, trustworthy and transparent is integral to maintaining a loyal customer base. However, putting a monetary value on all of the efforts that go into building that brand reputation can be difficult.

Both public relations and marketing have long struggled with quantifying results. Since most PR agencies focus almost exclusively on media relations, results have historically been measured by the number of media hits. Why is this a bad measurement? Two reasons.

First of all, these results have often been measured comparatively. If you're my client and I'm your agency, I might tell you that a half-page article written about you or your business in the WSJ is equal in value to a half-page advertisement. This is a common practice in public relations and is referred to as advertising value equivalency (AVE).

If you have any experience purchasing advertising space in the WSJ, you know that the cost is astronomical, so in many cases, no, that article is not as valuable as the advertisement. But in some cases, it might be just as valuable. Hell, it might be more valuable! The only thing we know for sure is that it's not the same thing. Apples and oranges. Bad metrics. Second of all, even if you have an agreed upon value of what a media hit in a specific outlet is worth to you, why stop there? That's such a surface-level measurement.

Through Google Analytics and other accurate tools, we're able to measure the effects of media attention and overall public relations efforts in ways never before possible. Let's go back to that half-page article in the WSJ example. Instead of providing you with the AVE or simply reporting that the article is live, we can and should be asking many questions, including:

— How many people were directed to our website from that post?
— What percentage of them turned into paying customers?
— Was our target demographic represented in the referred traffic?
— How many people shared the post with their social networks?
— Was the reaction positive?

All of this information is now available and allows us to answer the tough questions with data rather than instincts. A lot of the change that occurred in advertising from the Mad Men days to today, where decisions are (usually) based on data, can be attributed to new tools and ways to measure what the public wants. Just like advertising evolved with technology, so must public relations.

Guest Blogging Done Right

Guest blogging gives you the ability to build credibility, links pointing to websites and social profiles, social following, community, industry relationships, visibility, increased traffic, and more. It's one of the many ways to make a name for yourself in an industry, promote your business, and build a community.

This chapter is contributed by Brian Honigman, a guest blogging dynamo and tech writer for Mashable, Huffington Post, Entrepreneur, Forbes, and the Next Web. Here's his advice on making this powerful credibility-building tactic work.

Guest Blogging Best Practices

When it comes to guest blogging it's important to build relationships with other bloggers and editors. Once you're pitching and contributing to another website, you want to create content that's of value to your audience and the audience that typically reads the content on the website you're contributing to. It's important to match the style and guidelines of the blog you're contributing to, whether that means they prefer articles on a certain subject, of a certain word count, etc.

SEO Toolbox: Use **SocialCrawlytics** to analyze the best performing content of the blog you want to write for. Identify the most shared blog posts and refer to them in your outreach to its editor, pitching to write similar content.

Create quality content that includes a bio about yourself with links to your relevant properties, whether that's your own blog, social accounts, a link to your new book, or a link to your upcoming webinar. Always ask yourself: "Is this post of value to whom I'm trying to reach?"

Most importantly, you aren't going to find success with three articles you've contributed to other websites. It's a long-term commitment that won't start to drive results for yourself until you've gotten a large quantity of quality articles out there. Start with three and expand to 30 guest blogs, and then continue from there.

By consistently covering certain subjects over time, you'll be considered an expert on those topics. I've also learned more about what headlines resonate the best with readers across different blogs and publications.

I found an interesting tool from Portent's **Idea Generator** helpful in directing how I structure a headline for an article, which has helped match them more effectively with the interests of my audience and make them more engaging to click on in the search engines and across social media.

Finally, I've learned that making the most of a guest blogging opportunity doesn't end when the article is published but continues in how the post is distributed, how relationships are built over time, and how you continue to foster a community. For instance, answering comments on your articles will help continue to drive conversations about your articles over time, since readers know you're there to have an ongoing dialogue, whether it's in the comments of an article or on Twitter.

How to Land High-Value Guest Blogging Gigs

You need to continually write content on your own website, as well as guest blog on lesser-known websites in your industry. Once you've written a number of quality posts on your properties, as well as on other third-party websites, you can start to pitch bigger, more popular, and more exclusive publications. When I first started guest blogging I contributed to websites like AllFacebook and Social Times, which are high-traffic websites with less popularity than some of the larger, more well-known blogs. They were a great way to get my name out there and continue to drive value for others in our industry.

In your pitch, share what topics you'd like to cover, as well as examples of your content on other websites in the industry, whether that's the blog of another blogger or on a smaller publication. This gives you more credibility when you're trying to pitch a larger website like Mashable or Forbes.

The Decay of Guest Blogging for SEO

One cannot discuss guest blogging without referencing Matt Cutt's (the head of Google's WebSpam team) latest announcement on his blog, MattCutts.com:

"Okay, I'm calling it: if you're using guest blogging as a way to gain links in 2014, you should probably stop. Why? Because over time it's become a more and more spammy practice, and if you're doing a lot of guest blogging then you're hanging out with really bad company.

Back in the day, guest blogging used to be a respectable thing, much like getting a coveted, respected author to write the introduction of your book. It's not that way any more."

Furthermore, Matt Cutts shared an example of an unsolicited, spam email that he *himself* received from a black hat SEO. I decided to publish it in its entirety so that you can really understand how the good guest blogging Brian is talking about is different from what Google refers as to as 'guest blogging for SEO.'

> My name is XXXXXXX XXXXXXXX and I work as a content marketer for a high end digital marketing agency in [a city halfway around the world]. I have been promoting high quality content in select niches for our clients.
>
> We are always on the lookout for professional, high class sites to further promote our clients and when I came across your blog I was very impressed with the fan following that you have established.I [sic] would love to speak to you regarding the possibility of posting some guest articles on your blog. Should you be open to the idea, **we can consider making suitable contribution**, befitting to high standard of services that your blog offers to larger audience.
> On my part, I assure you a high quality article that is-
>
> - 100% original
> - Well written
> - Relevant to your audience and
> - Exclusive to you
>
> We can also explore including internal links to related articles across your site to help keep your readers engaged with other content on your blog.
>
> All I ask in return is a **dofollow link or two in the article body** that will be relevant to your audience and the article. We understand that you will want to approve the article, and I can assure you that we work with a team of highly talented writers, so we can guarantee that the article would be insightful and professionally written. We aim to write content that will benefit your loyal readers. We are also happy to write on any topic, you suggest for us.

You can't blame Matt Cutts for getting irritated with the Bad and the Ugly of the SEO community. The lesson here is this: if you don't play by the rules, you're going to get your wrist slapped by Google.

"Ultimately, this is why we can't have nice things in the SEO space: a trend starts out as authentic. Then more and more people pile on until only the barest trace of legitimate behavior remains. We've reached the point in the downward spiral where people are hawking "guest post outsourcing" and writing articles about "how to automate guest blogging."

What does it mean? Google is cracking down on spammy guest blogging practices. What you need to do is continue to provide quality content on your own website and on the websites you're contributing to reap the full benefits of guest blogging without being penalized by the search engines.

Link Building Toolbox

To give your credibility a boost, connect with other bloggers as you dive into content creation. Fellow Bloggers, Podcasters, Newsletter Junkies, and YouTubers who dig your style (and like you) will link to your content. Fellow bloggers can also offer you interviews, and interviews can lead to great contextual inbound links.

Powerful Community Platforms

Content is not king. Forget what you've learned.

Content shared in the right communities can reach 'king' status if you know where to post it...

...and how to connect with fellow community members. Optimizing your content comes down to creating magnetic headlines for your content that resonate with a carefully-selected, targeted audience, and building relationships with community members.

Here are a couple of community sites you can leverage to build relationships with like-minded influencers in your space.

Kingged.com

Kingged is a content curation site developed by Kingsley. Kingged lays out content according to its niche. Scroll down the home page to target your niche. 'Kingg' helpful, targeted blog posts to vote up your fellow Kingged users. Read the post. Post a comment on both your blog and on Kingged.com, sharing your take in a thorough fashion. Add within the blog post a comment that you found the post and left a similar content on kingged.com to create unique content for your fellow bloggers and for the Kingged.com website.

Don't just jump on Kingged.com in an attempt to share links and promote your content. Try to engage the community first by providing value – "kingging" (up voting) great content, commenting, and sharing quality, relevant content to your audience. Give before you ask. Jab multiple times before you deliver the right hook.

Kingged community members are loyal, engaging users who will happily comment on and promote your posts to their targeted followings. Kingged rewards its users with a **ComLuv commenting system**.

Members can select 1 of 10 frequent blog posts to further optimize their content marketing campaign. If the chosen Kingged post resonates with one of your 10 prior blog posts, use the post selecting option to link up to this resonant post and drive targeted traffic to your blog.

Triberr.com

Dino Dogan and Dan Cristo founded Tribber to connect like-minded entrepreneurs through an engaging platform. After signing up for Triberr, ask to join niche-specific tribes to optimize your content (make sure to request membership). Active participants will easily gain invites into new tribes. Actively scan potential tribes to find good matches for your niche of choice.

Engage frequently. Chatty tribe mates have few issues getting their content shared to relevant followings. Be a generous Triberr community member. Share as many posts as possible to generate good content karma. Many users will freely promote a generous person.

You have the option to share content to your Twitter stream at set time intervals. If you've identified bloggers on Triberr with a constant stream of amazing content, you can put them on auto-share. Join only niche-specific tribes and comment on relevant blog posts to see the greatest returns for your content optimization campaign.

Sharing your content with a targeted, hungry, ever-growing audience leverages your presence quickly. Join each community today. Become an engaging user on Kingged.com, Blog Engage, and Triberr to build your brand. Promote users aggressively, share your content in the right spots, and comment on relevant blog posts to effectively optimize your content marketing campaign.

How Build a Vibrant Community on Triberr

Next, Paul Shapiro, SEO Director at Catalyst and Top 47 Blogger on Tribber, explains winning strategies on Triberr.

It is important to get into the right tribes with the right people. You want to get the right eyes on your content. You also want to be able to build relationship with its members. Triberr is platform for authors, for people, not blogs. For life and for business, human relationships should always be your number one priority.

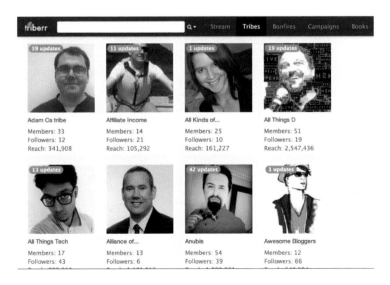

Also, you shouldn't feel obligated to Tweet out every blog post on Triberr. That would drive you crazy! Only share what you feel deserves to be shared and that is right for your audience. People will not be offended. They will be using the same methodology.

Triberr is also an excellent way to read interesting posts that you normally wouldn't come across. I often take the time to comment and read other people's writing, even if I am not sharing it on my social media channels. Again, it's about relationships above all else.

Other community sites I use include **BlogEngage.com**, **Inbound.org, Reddit.com**, and **GrowthHackers.com**.

Smart Outreach

As you build relationships in your industry, you can always rely on outreach to get more links to your content. When you develop great content and build strong relationships, outreach is a piece of cake. Good friends will help you spread the word when you reach out to them.

If link building outreach makes you uncomfortable, think about it more as value-exchange outreach. Traditional link building outreach consisted of sending email after email, asking for a link. Now you'll simply ask for people to share content that they like, for example by featuring your infographic, or by allowing you to guest post on their sites. It's all about **offering value**.

Your outreach techniques should blend with other forms of marketing, including:

  – Influencer relations
  – Social media
  – Co-marketing (best if done with companies larger than yours so you can ride on their coattails)
  – Digital media relations (which work wonderfully)

It took me quite some time to master email outreach. I usually only outreach asking for guest blogging opportunities; however, the techniques below can be used for any type of outreach:

  – Seek feedback (Brian Honigman offered me great tips)
  – Test different pitch copy
  – Keep it short (this is key; less is more)
  – Communicate value

– Build credibility
– Provide examples of your work

Here's an example of a cold outreach email that got me placements on The Next Web.

Tynt Publisher Tools

Tynt is a powerful tool to help increase SEO traffic. It's a widget that inserts your webpage URL when your content is copied and pasted into social networks, emails, and digital media outlets.

If you would like to see Tynt work for yourself, go to my website, click on any blog post, and copy any line of text. Paste anywhere and you'll see a link appear at the bottom of the content you copied that looks like this:

Read more: http://www.searchdecoder.com/8-internet-marketing-books-2014/#ixzz38c1VtJuR

The area I highlighted in gray is a URL tracking code generated by Tynt that allows you to track the offsite performance of your content so that you can get a cool performance report from Tynt that look like this:

searchdecoder.com 30 Day Overview

Last 30 days, Updated: July 23, 2014 04:19

Tynt actively monitored 5,035 page views.

Content Copies	New SEO Links	Incremental Traffic
388	**3**	**11**
Number of times content left your site.	Tynt generated links with SEO value.	Pageviews generated by Tynt links.

Rank	Page Title	URL Copies	Text Copies	Image Copies	Total Copies
1	Social Networks in China: 10 Marketing Tips How to Win on Sina Weibo	0	99	9	108
2	8 Internet Marketing Books You Should Read in 2014	0	52	4	56
3	Growth Hacker	Inbound Marketer	Matthew Capala	0	14	2	16

Here are some Key Benefits of using Tynt (via tynt.com):

Improving SEO rankings. When users copy and paste content into blogs, web sites or social networks, Tynt's CopyPaste auto-inserts the page URL, creating organic backlinks that can improve search rankings.

Driving incremental traffic. By inserting the page URL into shared content, Copy/Paste lets users click through to view the full content on your site. Tynt drives up to 20% more visits to individual web pages, and also increases traffic to your Facebook and Twitter pages through optional Follow Us links that can be inserted into copied content.

Getting actionable editorial insight. Discover opportunities for new content by analyzing the keywords and topics that drive users away from your site. Uncover topics that readers find highly engaging but lack visibility on your site.

Enhancing your user experience. Tynt makes it easy for users to reference your full web page. Ability to include custom links within the copied content.

Getting credit for your content. Tynt ensures that your brand travels with your content wherever it's pasted, encouraging users to source your content when sharing via copy & paste.

Link Analysis Toolbox

Open Site Explorer. Provides you with the ability to view the sites that are linking back to your website so you can strengthen your authority for better search engine rankings. A Pro membership is available, providing users with comprehensive applications to further analyze data.

Majestic SEO. Boasts the largest public index of its kind that provides comprehensive information on links, backlinks, domains, and keywords. Both free and paid registration options are available through the website.

Ahrefs. Fosters site optimization through link, anchor text, and keyword analysis based on its own independent crawler and index which updates every 15 minutes on average. Monthly subscription plans are available for more thorough reports.

Ravens Tools. Houses a vast array of strategic SEO, social media, and advertising tools to strengthen your website's online presence. A 30-day free trial is available along with optimized memberships that can be integrated with Google Analytics accounts.

Link Detective. Finds high quality and contextual links competitors are using through semantic markups and URL conversions to aid clever link-building.

Link Research Tools. The LRT platform has a variety of tools that tell you which links you need to get to beat the competition.

Part 4: CONNECTIONS

SOCIAL MEDIA

+ COMMUNITY

Content. Code. Credibility. They're essential, but to achieve true visibility on the Internet, you need Connections, our 4th 'C.'

Today, being connected is synonymous with having a presence on social networks such as LinkedIn, Facebook, Twitter, and Google Plus. These networks can be used to build a tightly-knit, loyal community that wants to hear from you on a regular basis, (and hopefully wants to buy from you as well).

Social networks have also radically changed link-building. Just a few years ago, most webmasters asked for links via email. Today much of this process – sometimes all of it – happens on social media networks.

While social is a huge force today, due the sheer number of people on social networks, it's also clear that the links that come to your site from social networks don't convey SEO benefits in the same way that a link from the New York Times of the Wall Street Journal would. But to focus on this fact is to miss the most interesting part of this question, which is this:

"How can I convince an editor at the New York Times to link to me?"

Very often, the answer to this question begins on social media, in communities, groups, and forum areas where people meet, exchange information, and bond with each other.

Want to get connected? Read on. In this chapter, you'll be hearing from voices that have used social media successfully to increase the influence of their sites, as well as their own influence.

Winning on Social Media

The right approach to marketing on the Internet involves a wide range of disciplines: psychology, social science, and data analytics. But above all, you need to be 'native' to the platform you are communicating through.

Winning Social Media Strategies

Remember that trust is the number one social media currency. Stand out on social platforms by being human. Users gauge whether or not your social media profile is authentic or spammy. Can users trust you based on what you share with your audience?

Keep image and branding in mind at all times. You have a single chance to make a first impression on social sites. Make your first impression a powerful impact. Tell an enchanting, continual story. Weave your brand into the fabric of your story on all social media websites.

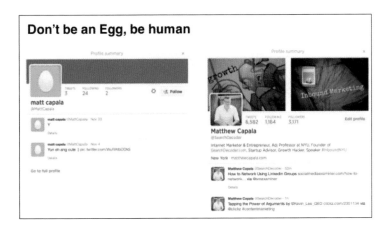

On sites like Twitter, upload a smiling, engaging image of yourself. Don't be an egg; be a human. Give users a chance to see who you really are so they can grow to know, like, and trust you.

Optimize each field on your social media profiles. Post a professional picture of yourself. Craft a descriptive, keyword-rich tagline. List your experience and education. Craft a short URL on sites like LinkedIn for a memorable reference and easier viewing.

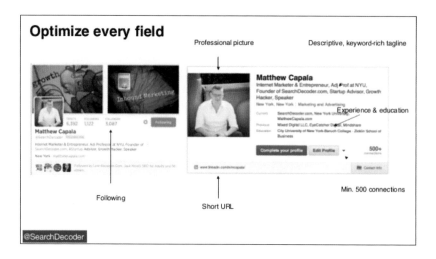

Do things, tell people. Follow this simple 1-2 punch to build your credibility on social media sites. Engage in chats and interviews to expand your presence. Make public speaking appearances and publish eBooks, blogs and podcasts to appear to be 'all over the web.' Boost your media mentions religiously.

Expose yourself to as many people across as many platforms as humanly possible. LinkedIn and SlideShare provide you with powerful content tools to build your brand and increase your visibility.

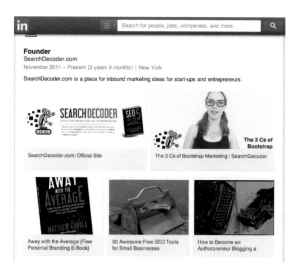

Make Friends Fast. Social media is about making friends quickly. Follow people, ask questions, and share answers to build friendship. Retweet, Like, and comment to pay it forward. Generous people quickly become popular on social media sites.

Think of the Golden Rule; give what you want. Follow others to be followed. Provide answers to prove that you are listening to your followers. Sharing answers inspires friends to ask you questions. If you want to be interesting, express genuine interest in others.

Think through how you can be of use to other people to become an influencer. Social media stars pay it forward in some way, shape, or form to become influential in their niche of choice.

Display Your Work Freely. Do not keep your accomplishments secret. You may just explode by hiding your work. Do things you like and don't fear telling your friends about it. Teach to learn more about a topic. If you need experience in any area, don't preach on what you don't know. Ask niche experts to explain concepts to you.

Create artful content. Patiently hone your craft to publish influential, compelling work which gets serious shares on social media sites.

Remember that intensity beats extensity. Focus your creative energies on playing to your strengths and use platforms, which naturally mirror your creative talents

The rise of the social media solopreneur

Gone are the days of huge, recognizable brands dominating social media marketing. Entertainment and information meld infotainment is the next gold rush. Solopreneurs are hopping onto the infotainment bandwagon by combining creativity with information-packed content to rise above social media noise.

Social media dynamo Gary Vaynerchuk has said: "Consumers don't want just information or just entertainment. They want infotainment."

Demand for infotainment has skyrocketed over the past 25 years. Consumers have been jaded by boring, listless presentations that are heavy on information and light on fluffy entertainment-laden messages. Brands who've found the right mix between the two have reached into the hearts and minds of sophisticated consumers.

Social Media Marketing: Lessons From the Boxing Ring

In his recent social media bestseller, "Jab, Jab, Jab, Right Hook," Gary Vaynerchuk tells marketers and businesses what boxing can teach them about marketing.

You should get the book, it's great, but let me explain how Gary illustrates social media marketing.

A boxer spends a lot of time analyzing his own strengths and weakness, as well as those of his opponent. When two boxers step into the ring, they already know each other well from countless hours of analysis and strategic planning. This step is crucial to win both in the ring and social media.

Effective boxers use a combination of jabs and right hooks to win the fight. A knock-out in boxing needs to be carefully set up by a series of jabs. It's no different than when you tell a good story; punch line has no power without the foundation that comes before it.

There is no sale without the story; no knockout without the setup. The right hook gets all the credit, but it's a series of well-planned jabs that come before it that set you up for success.

Right Hooks. Right hooks are the knockout punches. For marketers, those are the next highly anticipated campaigns that are going to increase revenue and make users engage in a cult-like following. A CMO's dream.

Right hooks are calls to action that benefit your business. They are meant to convert traffic into sales and ROI. Except when they don't....

Jabs. Jabs are a series of conversations, interactions and engagements, delivered one at a time, that slowly but authentically build relationships.

Jabs are the lightweight pieces of content that benefit your customers by making them laugh, snicker, ponder, play a game, feel appreciated, or escape.

Jab, jab, jab, right hook = give, give, give, ask.

Fortune 500 clients change their agencies frequently. Everyone is in constant pitch mode, planning the next right hook and trying to sell it to the c-suite.

It's a dog and pony show, cluttered with credentials and case studies. Marketing agencies compete on whose right-hook idea is the boldest. It's all about swinging hard knock-out punches that will take the brand 'to the next level.' That's your average social media strategy.

No one really talks about the jabs or what it takes to learn a platform. Or how to assemble a team that can respond in real-time to social media opportunities, such as Oreo's black-out campaign during

Super Bowl XLVII.

Here is the usual...

"Just throw all those ideas under the community management slide." What?

"There is a section about the social media dashboard in the back of the deck, you can put your ROI slide there." Thanks!

Big brands still get away with ignoring jabs because they can put large paid media budgets behind their right-hook campaigns. Facebook ads will bring needed traffic just fine. Look at all the Likes we got last time!

Most common end result: The campaigns reached the eyeballs. People saw them but they didn't care.

The chain reaction follows. Another RFP out. New strategy, bigger idea, more ad dollars. Another pitch, another agency, same outcome.

Know Your Platform, Act Like a User

Jumping on Reddit with your big marketing idea that worked great on Facebook may be disastrous. Why shouldn't you throw all your TV ads on YouTube? In theory, it sounds like a great idea to promote your services by answering questions on Quora.

You can't just throw your sales pitch and marketing material created for one platform, throw it up on another one, and then be surprised that people don't engage or are turned off by your efforts. You have to take the time to understand each platform and take a long view approach to developing a community.

If you want to become influential on the platform, you need to **act like the user**.

However, no matter how 'native' to the platform you are, your content has to be amazing. Effective social media marketing is about engaging your audience in compelling stories. That's a constant.

Gary's little dirty social media secret:

"Though I get to things early and can often see the future, I am not Nostradamus. I'm not even Yoda.* I'm just the kind of person who shows new platforms the respect they deserve. I won't predict what platform will see 20 million users in a year, but once it feels to me like it will, I will put my money and time there, testing new waters, trying new formulas, until I figure out how to best tell my story in a way the audience wants to hear it."

*It should read, 'Yoda I am not even,' should I point out.

Your number one job is to tell a story. No matter who you are or what you do, your number one job is to tell your story to the consumer wherever they are, and preferably at the moment when they are making decisions.

Adding a social media layer to any platform, especially SEO, increases its effectiveness. Social media is overtaking the search engines the same way TV overtook radio and the Internet overtook the newspaper. From now on, everything you do should have a social component.

There is no 60-day, there is only the 365-day marketing campaign, in which you produce content daily. Period.

Do not cling to nostalgia. Ignoring social media platforms that have gained critical mass is a sure way for a brand to look slow and out-of-touch.

Like boxers, great storytellers are observant and nimble. A great storyteller is keenly self-aware and attuned to his audience, he knows when to slow down for maximum suspense and when to speed up for comic effect. No boxer uses the same sequence of moves over and over again.

A story is at its best when it's non-intrusive. On social media, the only story that can achieve business goals is one told with native content. If you want to talk to people when they consume entertainment, you need to be entertainment. It doesn't require you to alter your brand identity — you shouldn't.

Content for the sake of content is pointless. Businesses are on social media because they want to be relevant and engaged, but if their content is banal and unimaginative, it only makes them look lame.

Content is king, but context is God. Even great content that goes onto your social channels can fall flat if you ignore the context of the platform on which it appears.

In summary, getting people to hear your story on social media and act on it requires:

 — using a platform's native language;
 — paying attention to context;
 — understanding the nuances and subtle differences that make each platform unique;
 — and adapting your content to match.

Marketers who understand social platforms at that fluid level will succeed. Get out there. Be human. Take the time to understand each platform and act like a user. Talk to people in ways that are native to the platform and you will win.

Social Media Automation: HootSuite

Another dirty little secret about social media is that it's labor-intensive. Just because social media uses short-form content doesn't mean that you don't have to put thought into it or check links in the same way you would with a blog article. But automated tools can ease some of the workload.

I had not used any social media tool until recently, when I realized how much time I can save automating content sharing and management of various social networks. HootSuite is a social media management system for businesses and individuals to execute social media campaigns across multiple social networks from one secure, web-based dashboard. You can streamline workflow with scheduling and invite multiple collaborators to manage social networks securely, plus provide custom reports using the comprehensive social analytics tools for measurement.

While I personally do not schedule my sharing often, I see many benefits for businesses of scheduling your social content calendar through a platform such as Hootsuite or **Buffer**. Social media scalability doesn't imply looking like a robot — maintain a fair balance of 'native' tweeting, sharing, asking, responding and 'scheduling' content to be shared.

I manage two Twitter accounts so Hootsuite comes handy for me.

Multiple accounts   Cross posting

Integrated dashboard

Social Connections in Action

You may not realize how powerful your social media network is until you reach out to it. For example, when I was writing this book I needed to reach out for help in the form of editorial contributions and feedback on important content issues.

I put some of my concerns out to my social network and didn't expect much of a response at first. But I was surprised by how many great people reached out to me in return. Human beings have a powerful instinct to help each other. Reach out to your own network – you may be as surprised as I was by the helpful spirit that can be present in a real community!

A lot of people who should know better have complained that "social media doesn't work," but that's just because they're looking at social in exactly the wrong way: as yet another place for them to yell out their marketing messages to the multitudes (who they apparently presume will not only accept but cheer this behavior on in the forms of Likes and Retweets.

Being effective on social media means rethinking your whole approach to communications to take account of the fact that in today's world, customers are in control, and brands need to learn to listen – not just preach.

One person who's got a lot to say on this topic is Brooke Ballard, in-the-trenches digital marketer and owner at B Squared Media. Do yourself a favor and read the following article, which can save you (or your agency, if you work for one) a ton of trouble when it comes to marketing on social media networks.

Think conversation, not campaign

If you really want to start understanding your audience, you need to know what drives them and what their buying behaviors are. You can't do this by sharing kitten memes or quotes, and you certainly can't do this by only allowing for one-way conversation.

What are the common social media pitfalls? The #1 most common (fatal) mistake I see with companies is planning to fail. What I mean by that is that they don't have a formal strategy or plan for their social media efforts, and without one their messaging will probably not be heard over the noise. Constantly sharing memes is not a strategy. Talking about yourself won't work. Selling aggressively is laughable. Coming up with some sort of viable plan for both relationship building and building your lists is the way to go.

Other common social media pitfalls are:

 – Spelling and grammar errors (this is probably a close 2nd!)

- Linking social media sites to "save" time
- Signing up for sites and then never posting there
- Using every social media network
- Not knowing the difference between tone and voice
- Not interacting with your communities)
- Not humanizing your brand
- Jargon speak
- Not sharing value

How to build a following on social networks? We find companies have the 'shiny object syndrome' and want to be on every platform. We encourage them to get focused, and choose only three platforms to start. Messaging gets diluted or redundant when you're on Facebook, LinkedIn, Pinterest, Instagram, Twitter, SnapChat, Foursquare, Google+, etc..

It's also important to choose the networks that complement your business. If you're B2B, that may be LinkedIn and Twitter. If you're selling a visual product or service, Instagram and Pinterest are good places to start.

Identify where your brand best fits first, and then take a look at where your target users spend their time. This will ensure you're able to grow a decent following on your chosen platforms.

We also don't get mired in the numbers. Vanity metrics are where amateurs focus – relationships and conversions are where your focus should be.

How to convert followers to community? If you really want to start understanding your audience, you need to know what drives them and what their buying behaviors are. You can't do this by sharing kitten memes or quotes, and you certainly can't do this by only allowing for one-way conversations.

It's kind of like dating. You have to "woo" your target customers with good content. You have to prove you're more valuable than the next guy/girl. And you must show them you care.

Two-way conversation also means responding to negative comments. You'd be surprised at how many companies stick their head in the sand by ignoring or deleting less-than-stellar feedback.

An Oracle report found that 79% of those that complained about customer service (online) had their complaints ignored.

Those complaints — as well as the good stuff — are your ticket to finding out exactly what consumers want from you ... firsthand!

Why use psychographic research for social media?

Psychographics — beliefs, opinions, feelings, values — can only be extracted through conversation. Scratch that. Psychographics can only be extracted when both parties are vulnerable, trustworthy, and accepting. If you, or your brand, is not those things then you will probably have a hard time getting people to share self disclosures with you – even if the conversation is flowing.

Imagine, though, being able to take the feelings of your community and put them to work for your brand. When you know things like values and opinions, you can make direct correlations with buying patterns.

Psychographics answer the question every marketer is trying to answer: "What do my buyers want?" So have more conversations. Woo your audience. Be dateable. Eventually you'll be able to ask psychographics-type questions and get answers.

How to measure return on social media investment? With social media, I don't think you can get to a ROI without a ROC.

ROI = Return on Investment and ROC = Return on Conversation.

"Can deeper interactions (garnering psychographics) and relationship building happen online (specifically on Facebook), between brands and consumers?"

The answer is YES.

However, to get to YES you're going to have to move past fluff and memes and get out of your comfort zone. You're going to have to think more deeply about the conversations you're having.

If everything you post on social media is cliché, your results will be cliche.

If you only share dull facts, you may only receive factual information in return.

If you push for opinions and feelings — and are sure to share your own — you may start to receive opinions and feelings from your community.

It's that simple.

Or maybe it's not. But if it isn't, I'm fearful of what may happen to your business as the Consumer Revolution continues to flourish.

The bottom line is that companies can no longer see consumers as dollar signs. They can't even view them as avatars or User1234. If they want to stay on top (and in business) they have to start building relationships with their connected communities.

Social Media Toolbox

Follower Wonk. A twitter intelligence tool that can be used to track and analyze followers, as well as search and find key influencers via twitter bios. Full analytical SEO and social tools can be accessed by subscribing monthly.

HootSuite. Manages social media and messaging on a dashboard that integrates your brand's social networks and apps. Customizable analytics are also available and at a minimal monthly fee, full features can be accessed.

Twitter Adder. An automated twitter system that is touted as a "time saver". It can be set up to manage multiple Twitter accounts, tweet, search for new followers based on chosen criteria, add and manage them.

Mention Map. An exciting web app for exploring your Twitter network. Discover which people interact the most and what they're talking about. It's also a great way to find relevant people to follow.

Rite Tag. RiteTag empowers you to identify the right #hashtags to get your message further, getting your content out to those who are passively and actively looking for it.

Topsy. Social search and social analytics combined in one indexed resource. Access, analyze and gain insight from years of Twitter conversations. This tool is also handy for measuring exposure, providing exact counts of terms and hashtags.

Social Crawlitics. Identify your competitor's most shared content and discover social media metrics behind each URL on your site.

Building Your Tribe

Google has a 'love affair' with websites that can demonstrate a strong community of users who contribute user-generated content (aka UGC) through publishing tools, forums, and commenting.

In my experience, there is no shortcut to community development. It's a grind, but your approach is far more important than how hard you hustle.

You cannot buy love on social media; you have to earn it.

Audience vs. Community. Attracting an audience and building a community are two different activities. Audience members are mere numbers in most cases. Think about the number of followers on Twitter. Communities support you and trumpet your brand to their followers. Think about the number of retweets on Twitter or answers to a questions you posted on Facebook.

Build a community through patience and persistence. Gaming the social media marketing system by buying "Likes" won't help you create an active, engaging following.

Seth Godin mentions in his book Tribes that "A tribe is a group of people connected to one another, connected to a leader, and connected to an idea." Connect with your followers and bind them into a community through a core idea.

If you want to develop a vibrant community when you are just starting out, focus on a specific niche and build your expertise in that area through thought leadership content, including blogging, ebooks, video tutorials, etc.

Participate religiously in forums and comment on other sites, more popular than yours, to build relationships by providing value. Eventually you gain influence and will be able to drive traffic to your website.

Once you start developing traffic to your site, introduce community tools, such as forums, and provide value by answering questions and moderating.

Require a signup so that you can collect emails to promote your info-products.

Repeat, learn, test. The formula is simple, consistency is hard.

Examples of strong community sites in the SEO world include Moz.com, so go check out what they are doing right.

Next I invited two user development hackers to share their experience building two high-growth start-ups.

Dan Cristo bootstrapped Triberr with his partner Dino Dogan from zero to over 70K users without any paid media dollars

Andrew Wond bootsrapped Coinvent (formerly NYEBN) from zero to 30K strong, and is now one of the most vibrant start-up communities in NYC on Meetup.com

User development do's and don'ts

by Dan Cristo, Co-Founder of Triberr, Director of Innovation at Catalyst

Imagine a man running through a forest as fast as he absolutely can. He's pumped with adrenaline to the point where he's blazing through branches, tumbling down steep hills and scaling rocks with no fear and no pain. When faced with an obstacle he takes only seconds to come up with a solution and tries it until he succeeds. That's the spirit of developing user base when you are bootstrapping.

DO create a 'Coming Soon' page with an email subscribe area months before you launch.

DO launch in a closed Beta for as long as it takes to work the bugs out.

DO offer registration/sign in options for social media, such as Facebook, Twitter, LinkedIn and G+.

DO blog about your project updates, industry news and curate useful content.

DO email your entire member list at least once a month. It's a great way to stay top of mind, and there will be so many changes in a month's time they will like hearing about features you're adding next.

DON'T try to get a TechCrunch write-up right away. Your site likely isn't ready to scale quickly out the gate. A TC mention will send a flood of traffic to what is likely a half-baked site. Try to wait a year or so before pursuing major outlet mentions.

DON'T spend money on Adwords, banner ads or any form of marketing where you pay for traffic. Instead, spend your money on marketing tools such as MailChimp, Buffer, and WordPress themes where you can do the marketing yourself.

DON'T try to be on every social network. Choose one or two that you're actually going to invest time and energy on. Which two depends on your product, your audience, and your personal preference.

How to attract your first 1,000 followers

by Andrew Wong, Founder and CEO of Coinvent (Formerly NYEBN)

In order to build a powerful brand on a platform like **Meetup.com**, you must be unique and be prepared for the fact that building the first 500 or 1,000 users is likely to take some time. So it won't be a business from the get-go. You must have other businesses to supplement your income somehow during that initial period of time.

Keep in mind that community organizers live in public. So think twice before you take action. Once you are committed, you will be responsible and held accountable for your future actions.

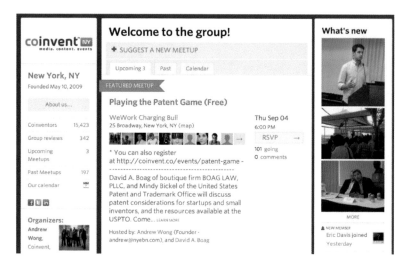

Enable your users to interact with each other. The network effort matters a lot! For example, NYEBN's Facebook page engages users with stories they like. NYEBN's Meetup message board lets users post news items and have discussions about them. The same goes with NYEBN's LinkedIn discussion forum.

Define your value proposition You must constantly give away value to keep growing your community. That means no BS talk. Everything you do must generate direct or indirect value to your users. Many community organizers fail because they put their personal agenda ahead of everything else.

Connecting Google + Authorship

This topic is usually covered as a small blurb in most textbooks and how-to guides. Make no mistake, Google has been very vocal about what type of signals it 'already started using' and website owners need to follow through to see their content in Google's search results.

That said, I decided to dedicate an entire chapter to what in SEO circles is referred to as **rel=author**.

Don't let the name scare you. You can hook up your Google+ authorship to your blog, or if you are guest blogging, to your author pages on the other blogs, in five minutes or less. I took couple screenshots to walk you through at the bottom of this chapter to make it a breeze.

In simple terms, authorship is how Google knows that an individual human published a blog post or an article. Google is trying to collect data on content creators so that its algorithms get smarter.

In order for Google to identify and return the best content to the user, Google needs to be able to:

#1 Figure out if the content is relevant to the user query;

#2 Use content performance signals, such as social sharing, commenting, and the number and quality of backlinks pointing to that content;

#3 Identify, learn about and rank content creators according to their perceived influence and thematic relevance.

Google+ Authorship (aka rel=author)

Connecting your Google+ profile with the work you publish online will help you increase your online influence, visibility and boost your SEO.

Why is it important to build and connect your author profile if you are blogging (or guest blogging)?

Google rewards verified online profiles and ranks better those bloggers who set up their authorship in Google+. If you are using multiple authors as guest bloggers, you need to set up G+ authorship for each user, which will in turn pass their online influence onto your blog.

Here is what Eric Schmidt, a former CEO and now Chairman of Google:

"Within search results, information tied to verified online profiles will be ranked higher than content without such verification, which will result in user naturally click on the top (verified results)...."

Not convinced yet?

"...so the true cost of remaining anonymous then, will be irrelevance."

Google organic search links with confirmed author profiles (indicated by the image along with the number of Google+ circles) receive about 30% higher click-through-rates.

30 Awesome Free SEO Tools for Small Businesses - Search...
www.searchdecoder.com/free-seo-tools-for-small-businesses/ ▾
by Matthew Capala - in 103 Google+ circles
Sep 15, 2013 - ... to your business. Use for keyword search volume analysis.
.... **How to Leverage the Power of Guest Blogging** to Win Big February 19, 2014.

How to Connect Google+ Authorship to Your Blog Posts

To link your blog posts to Google Authorship you must first log in (or create) a Google Plus profile.

#1 Go to the "Account" page of your G+ profile;

#2 Click on the "Edit Profile" link;

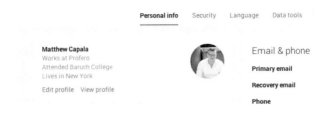

#3 Find the section called "Links" and click "Edit;" and select "Contributor to."

#4 Click "Add custom link" in the "Contributor to" section & name it with the blog name you are writing for in the "Label" field;

#5 Add the URL of your author profile to the URL field (example: https://blog.com/author/username);

#6 Click Save;

#7 Locate the User settings in your blogging platform (below is an example of how to locate it in WordPress) and click "Edit;"

#9 When you access the "Edit" under your User profile and find where you need to enter your Google+ URL, which should look like this: https://plus.google.com/+MatthewCapala/

If you are using a third-party blogging platform, you need to identify your **user settings** and perform this step. If you are guest posting, contact the blog owner/webmaster to connect your G+ profile (you still need to perform the first 8 steps).

#10 Go to Google's **Structured Data Testing Tool** and test it to make sure your authorship is connected properly.

Structured Data Testing Tool

| URL | HTML |

http://www.searchdecoder.com/leverage-power-guest-blogging/   [PREVIEW]   Examples ▾

Select the HTML tab to view the retrieved HTML and experiment with adjusting it.

Google search results   Google Custom Search

Preview

How to Leverage the Power of Guest Blogging to Win Big |
www.searchdecoder.com/leverage-power-guest-blogging/
by Matthew Capala
The excerpt from the page will show up here. The reason we can't show text from
your webpage is because the text depends on the query the user types.

Authorship Testing Result

Authorship is working for this webpage.

Google+ profile link: https://plus.google.com/101024478095670924065
Google+ profile name: **Matthew Capala**
Your authorship setup is finished. Congratulations! However, please note that Google will only show your author portrait in search results
user. Learn more

Done!

3 Niche Social Networks for Big Results

There is more to social media than Facebook and Twitter. Target emerging social platforms for high-growth opportunities.

Consider your skills and the following factors when choosing the social networks you can achieve highest growth for your efforts.

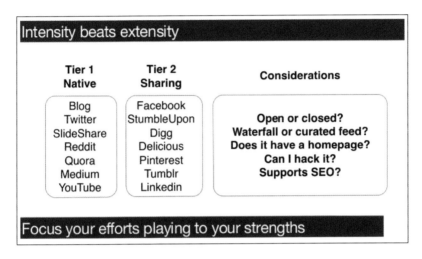

Below are a couple of social networks that can bring you big results, including:

#1 Slideshare;

#2 Reddit;

#3 Quora.

Tell Stories on SlideShare

Have you used SlideShare? It is a slide hosting platform — similar to YouTube, but for slideshows. With 60 million monthly visitors and 130 million page views, it is among the 200 most visited websites in the world.

SlideShare has been very generous for me. The graphic marketing tool can turbocharge your business or personal brand. Serving up images relevant to the brand you are trying to build, combined with short, punchy text, sends out an irresistible message to learn more about you.

If you do not prefer writing in-depth posts or mugging for videos SlideShare can be your online savior. It is also a great medium for introverts interested in self-promotion or businesses with zero design skills (assuming that you know PowerPoint) because you don't need to get in front of the camera or a big audience or create advanced designs.

Storytelling rules on SlideShare. Stories never go out of style. Build a story through a combination of colorful imagery and eye-catching copy to reel in intrigued viewers and expand your brand awareness.

Show off your talents while weaving an inspiring tale for viewers. Since storytelling brands rule the online and offline world you would be wise to follow branding wizards and case studies on the subject.

I want to share the branding process I have tested on SlideShare that generated over 200K views for me last year and over 300K in under two years, so you can start to think about positioning yourself for success on this growing platform. This process also helped me become top 1% influencer on SlideShare.

Craft a slogan. Dwell on the idea that best describes you. Build your SlideShare presentation on this slogan to resonate with your target audience. Observe the most well-known brands and influencers for inspiration. Your calling card might be solving specific problems faced by people in your niche.

I took a strategy of being a bit mysterious. As I was growing my influence, I wanted to introduce my brand to people who didn't know me, thus 'Who is SearchDecoder?'

Make sure to include a professional photo to connect with your target audience. Build a trustworthy, personable brand by literally allowing your online audience to see you. Few forms of online content disarm web visitors as well as a smiling, professional head shot.

Explain what you do...visually. People need to know how you can help them. Explain what you do before describing who you are. Powerhouse brands weave an enchanting story around how the brand can benefit individuals. Be the benefit. Describe how you can help your viewers.

Describe your services so potential customers can envision how your skills match solutions to their problems. Be as explicit as possible to create clarity in the mind of your prospects.

List services and credentials. Stand out from your crowded niche by sharing your credentials. What makes you special? What makes you tick?

If you are a professional, showcase your experience and former clients or companies you've worked at.

Share Examples of Your Work. Let SlideShare viewers kick the tires and take your work for a test run before deciding to hire you. Share your work to give potential leads a glimpse into your finished product. Your work represents your brand. Post images of your finest masterpieces to resonate strongly with your ideal client.

Show any extracurricular or non-profit projects that will emphasize your cause-leadership attitude. It's important in work and life.

Tap into the most powerful form of advertising on earth: word of mouth marketing. People might not believe you initially but are likely to trust glowing, authentic testimonials presented by their friends. Post slides of your best customer testimonials to build your brand on solid ground.

Go Off Topic. Why? Easy. People want to partner with a human. Humans do stuff outside of business, like taking vacations, or engaging in hobbies like skydiving. Say something interesting about yourself to strengthen your brand and connect with your audience. Post light, fun slides of you doing stuff outside of biz-related tasks.

Engage with a Call-to-Action. Offer something for free you could charge for and direct users to your website where you can convert them into audience, leads, and clients.

Post Contact Information. Make it easy for people to connect with you by creating a slide listing your contact information. Include your phone number, email address, cell phone, Skype number and social media accounts on the slide. Allow viewers to reach you through their channel of choice. Gain the trust of your target market by being transparent.

Be original and do things you haven't seen before. Talk about it, share lessons and wins. Document your process.

Embrace the Internet Culture on Reddit

Next, Clayburn Griffin, Founder of the BigSEO subreddit on Reddit, and Content Strategist at 360i, explains how to leverage Reddit for big results.

Reddit is Internet culture. It is everything from a Q&A site to a support group to a porn site. Marketers need to understand it before they engage in spam, which tends to be their first instinct on Reddit. You can read reports and do some research, but immersing yourself in the Reddit community is the best way to "get it".

Why should Reddit be a part of your SEO strategy? There is a lot that Reddit has to offer that is particularly helpful to people in marketing, especially those who work in the world of online marketing. It's also very much the product of this generation.

It's apparent in politics, with a progressive President hip to social media. Television is trying in many ways to figure out how to adapt. The music industry was caught off guard and soon found ways of coping, though they still haven't fully recovered.

And Reddit is the easiest place for you to be a part of that change and see it happening and who's making it happen. Any new sensation or idea will make its way onto Reddit and the community at large will react. Keep your eye on it or you'll be like a dinosaur: extinct.

How to succeed on Reddit? It depends on your goals. Why are you using Reddit? I would suggest that there are a few goals you haven't considered, such as keeping on top of pop culture and definitely Internet culture. It can challenge you and your beliefs. It can help you find and interact with interesting people. It can teach you about almost any subject. You have to look at it as more than potential website traffic, which can be hard for us SEOs.

Find the right subreddits. A good start to look for lists of trending subreddits you can find on **stattit.com** and **redditmetrics.com**. There's also a subreddit for finding subreddits! Making sure you're in the right place is definitely step #1.

Speak Reddit's language. As corny as it is (and maybe because it's corny) many Redditors like to refer to Reddit in third-person as a collective. "What does Reddit think of the picture my 84-year old grandma drew on her new iPad?" There are in-jokes you can reference and figures of speech or abbreviations like "tl;dr" (too long; didn't read) and "afaik" (as far as I know).

Provide value. That's something that should be true of anything you do when involving others. When you strike up a conversation with a co-worker, are you just wasting their time or do you have something interesting or important to say? If you're going to pay millions for an ad during the Super Bowl, will the audience enjoy it and is your product something they would want?

Sometimes marketers are too focused on what they want from

people and forget to think about what they have to offer. If you can't answer what value you're providing, then people will resent you wasting their time. The Internet, and especially Reddit, is impatient and has a short attention span.

Develop the thick skin. Reddit audience can be 'brutally' honest. I think it's important to be open to negative feedback. You'll probably get some on Reddit. It's almost inevitable. And sometimes they're right. You have to become good at listening and understanding what points are valid. As an aspiring writer, I often put my stuff out to be critiqued by people.

The response I get requires consideration. I can't blindly accept all criticism. I have to think about what the person is saying, and why. Maybe they interpreted the piece differently than what I meant. What can I change to make my point more clear? You have to apply critical thinking to all criticism.

Tap Into the Power of Quora

Next Amrita Saha, my former NYU student and digital marketing professional, talks about how tap into a huge traffic potential Quora.com has to offer.

We are social animals, no doubt about it! And we value the opinions of others. That's why we are always keen to search for information on Google before making any type of decision. If you are one such animal, then Quora is the right place for you. It is likely to be the site to go to receive opinions and most importantly, answers to those questions that bubble in our minds daily. Simplistically described, Quora is a question-and- answer online forum.

To give it a try myself, I asked Quora: 'What is the future of Pinterest?'

Here's what I found.

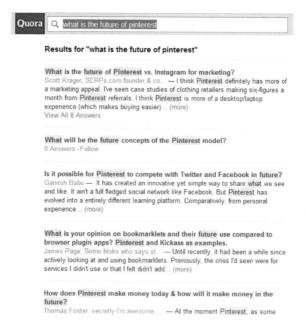

In addition to the answer that I was looking for, I also found many other questions that were related to the same topic, answers from various people, as well as different perspectives related to Pinterest.

How Quora is Different

On Quora, your main identity is your interests and your expertise.

Your friends can see what topics you are interested in, and what questions you are answering. You gain status by having a well phrased answer that properly addresses the question. You can follow people you find insightful and through them you find new people.

Sounding similar to the popular websites? Indeed, but Quora seems to be different in a way that is best described by a series of metaphors:

Quora is like Yahoo! Answers...but instead, the same questions and answers are continually being edited, reviewed, and added to. It comes with a user friendly interface, which focuses on the real identities of users, and has no limited window to answer questions.

Quora is like Google...but instead, you get your answer from subject matter experts along with different views and explanations; instead of various and sometimes low-quality links to the same question.

Quora is like Facebook...but instead, you follow categories of interest and topics versus people such as friends and family. Your main identity is defined by your knowledge and expertise, instead of your profile page where you upload photos and your friends post on your wall.

Quora is like Wikipedia...but instead, it answers your specific question rather than being just an encyclopedia. It provides a mechanism for social and interest-specific, real-time distribution of information. Quora effectively supports multiple points of view, discussions, and allows you to get to know other respondents.

In short, Quora's uniqueness comes from the fact that users have the ability to seek information independently, by asking a question that is tailored exactly to what they want to know. Its biggest strength and what sets it apart from its competitors is its ability to act as a focused crowdsourcing clearinghouse. The ability to follow topics and questions in a niche, allows it to be a great market research tool.

How Businesses Can Benefit from Quora

It's important to note that Quora currently won't let brands or companies set up organizational profiles, however there are a few exceptions. One of the better ways to participate is through the profile of a high-ranking executive or spokesperson. Below are 6 ways your company can benefit from using Quora.

Monitoring. Quora can provide a monitoring platform for your business. Whenever a question is posted that is related to your business, you can tap into the interest generated instantly. Your designated Quora user can also respond to the query and also create the much needed eminence.

Relationship building. Quora is quickly gaining the status of the new social media sensation. Its user friendly interface allows you get a sense of the most active participants within a topic area.

Research and Feedback. With an active base of participants who follow or at least are interested in your company or products, Quora also offers a platform for soliciting feedback for use in product design, marketing or other strategies.

Brand Awareness. Quora is gaining a lot of attention among the start-up and small business community for its unique social sharing feature, combined with the question-and-answer format that enables easy communication between users. The more you share and participate within your network, the higher becomes the chance of more people knowing about your business.

To start using Quora, simply ask or answer a question today.

5: CASH

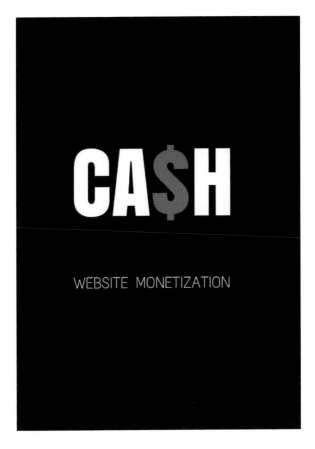

Congratulations again. You've made it through the gristle and meat of the SEO process. You've learned about how important it is to provide great content, demonstrate your credibility, and be connected to a community.

Now it's time to talk money. After all, it's all about the Benjamins!

But wait just one moment more. Before you dive into the specific monetization tactics listed in this chapter, take a deep breath and a big step back. Fear not: money awaits those who heed the following pieces of advice:

Practice detachment. Detach from money outcomes to build your SEO campaign on a solid foundation at the outset. However, form a clear monetization strategy on day one, using metrics such as newsletter list growth, which is the foundation of every healthy monetization scheme.

Don't hard sell before you won trust and credibility. You may be in business, where boosting immediate cash flow is a primary goal. But detaching helps you take the proper steps to best connect with your ideal reader and client.

Ask for the subscriber's name and email address, before you ask them to open up their wallets. You need to build an intelligent, multi-stage approach to making money through your online endeavors. Offering free, useful and targeted content primes the monetization pump. Give away free ebooks and other useful products to build your email list.

Sell helpful products through your email newsletter after you've offered serious value for a sustained period of time. Lead with value to receive value. Lead with solid, usable content to receive value in the form of money.

Sharing free, valuable content inspires subscribers to know, like and trust you. Once you've done this, they will *want* to buy from you.

5 Website Monetization Models

Every website should be built with 'monetization' in mind.

However you sell, convince, generate buzz, promote yourself, or generate leads for your offline business, you need to identify appropriate website success metrics that are tied to your short-term and long-term goals, and ultimately, to making money.

There are essentially five e-business website models that most websites engage in. They are not exclusive – you should always consider setting multiple income streams for your online endeavors.

In one form or another, I leverage all of the models listed below on my website.

The Brochure Model. Here, your website functions as a business card or brochure for your offline business. You want your site visitors to either visit your brick-and-mortar store or contact you. The monetization objectives for a brochure website are to drive store traffic or business leads.

Make sure to include intuitive site navigation, with an objective to funnel users to the 'contact us' page. Feature strong calls-to-action on your website that will drive your visitors to call you (e.g. free consultation). When you get a lead, make sure to ask how your visitor found you.

The Subscription Model: Your website offers high-quality, exclusive content that users are drawn to and are either willing to pay for directly or are willing to divulge information for (typically an email address and/or phone number) that lets you build a subscriber list for your email marketing efforts.

Whatever your monetization model, it's wise to constantly build your list through giveaways and smart promotions. Include prominent calls to action on your website to capture new subscribers daily.

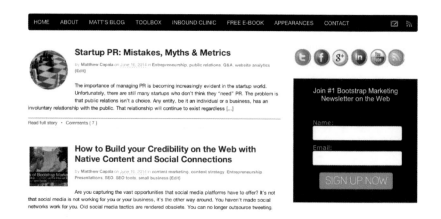

Use email and list management such as **AWeber** or **MailChimp** to effectively manage your newsletter campaigns. Include links to your content in your Newsletter to cross-promote your content.

Don't sweat purchasing expensive newsletter designs or templates before you get more than a couple of thousand email subscribers. I still use **plain text,** as do some of the biggest newsletter gurus out there. Don't obsess over the form of your email; rather focus on the value you are proving to your readers. Never spam.

The Advertising Model: Your website offers great content and you've developed an engaged audience and a steady flow of traffic. Here, you simply sign up with an ad network such as **Google Adsense**, and place ads on your website like the two ad units you can view below.

When users click on those ads, you make cash. But be advised that you won't make a lot of cash unless your site gets a lot of traffic.

The E-Commerce Model: Your website has a shopping cart and you sell directly. Pretty self-explanatory. If you're looking to build an ecommerce site, consider **Shopify**, a tool that lets anybody build a simple shopping experience. However, you may do better leveraging platforms like Amazon and Ebay that already have large audiences you can tap into to get discovered.

The Affiliate Model: Your website promotes products through affiliate marketing. Affiliate marketing is a type of performance-based marketing in which a business rewards one or more affiliates for each visitor or customer brought by the affiliate's own marketing efforts.

There are many affiliate networks you can join, the largest being **Commission Junction** (now CJ Affiliate). Some sites also offer a direct affiliate relationship, which will usually get you a much higher share of profit.

Affiliate marketing can be tricky because participants are somewhat motivated to promote higher-priced items with high commission rates. So make sure you only recommend the products you use and love.

I currently only use the **Amazon Affiliate Network** for the books I often recommend to my readers.

	Impressions	Clicks	CTR	Rank
internet marketing books	329	24	7%	5.1
online marketing books	211	21	10%	5.3
best marketing books 2014	244	19	8%	7.7
best online marketing books	116	18	16%	5.8
online marketing book	307	16	5%	5.7
weibo marketing	48	16	33%	3.5
online marketing books 2014	22	16	73%	1.3
best online marketing books 2014	23	15	65%	1.3
how to use quora	123	13	11%	6.2
best internet marketing books	107	13	12%	5.8
books on online marketing	49	13	27%	4.6
best internet marketing books 2014	14	13	93%	1.4
internet marketing book	145	11	8%	5.1
books on internet marketing	51	11	22%	4.0

Don't expect to make a fortune this way. Amazon offers 4-6% commissions for every book they sell, so you can do the math. However, a smart monetization strategist always diversifies his income streams. The key principle in making money online is that **small things will compound** if you are persistent and stick to it. You have to play a long-term game.

Because my content ranks highly on Google on keywords such as 'online/internet marketing books,' I get a steady flow of highly-targeted traffic. That's called **passive income**.

Earnings Report Totals			Glossary
	Items Shipped	Revenue	Advertising Fees
Total Amazon.com Items Shipped	75	$1,157.15	$69.67
Total Third Party Items Shipped ①	61	$650.13	$39.49
Total Items Shipped	**136**	**$1,807.28**	**$109.16**
Total Items Returned	**-13**	**-$78.32**	**-$3.14**
Total Refunds	**0**	**$0.00**	**$0.00**
TOTAL ADVERTISING FEES	123	$1,728.96	$106.02

By the way, if you are curious about which books I recommend for marketers to read, you can find my book list at: searchdecoder.com/8-internet-marketing-books-2014/

You shouldn't hide or conceal the fact that you have affiliate relationships with networks or sites like Amazon. Learn from passive income gurus, such as Pat Flynn, and put trust and ethics in front of short-term profits.

Check out Patt's Monthly Passive Income Reports to learn the tricks of the monetization trade at SmartPassiveIncome.com.

Making Money With Your Blog

If you think you can't make money with your blog, you've been listening to the wrong people. Listen now to Ryan Biddulph, who turned his blog into a major revenue source and changed his whole life for the better. Ryan, a former fired security guard in New Jersey, is currently a world traveler and blogger. He went from having a net worth of 4 cents to generating a steady cash flow online while living in tropical paradises like Bali, Phuket, and Hoi An.

Anybody can make money online 'if' they are willing to know exactly why they want to do so. This means developing a crystal-clear vision of what you want to do most. See yourself living your dreams, now, to fuel your drive.

Ryan's Current Location: Savusavu Fiji

Obstacles will arise along the path; most people fail to make money online because their fear of obstacles is stronger than their will to succeed. This crowd quits, but the people who make fortunes have a powerful desire to succeed online, usually tied to some form of freedom.

Money responds to value, both online and offline. Your content does the selling and your network amplifies your reach. Here is the tough part: your links and ads become clickable only after you have become an expert in your field.

If you want to make money online, focus on 2 core activities:

creating value and making friends.

Create value. Create valuable blog posts, videos, newsletters, and podcasts to become attractive to money. Give away free, valuable information to gain the trust of your target audience. People trust someone who's willing to offer valuable, helpful, free information persistently.

Target your ideal customer. Use keywords that these individuals would type into Google (or other search engines) throughout your content. Never go overboard; peppering keywords or key phrases a few times into a 600 word post should do the trick.

Make friends. Your network grows your net worth. Make friends to grow your network. If I retweeted my latest post 3 times today I might generate decent traffic. If 50 of my friends retweeted my latest post today I will see a flood of traffic.

Be a friend to make friends. Promote other people, comment on their blogs, and build strategic partnerships through social networking sites and email. Live the Golden Rule. Treat people in the same way you wish to be treated. Help others make money online and online money will flow into your coffers too.

Ninh Binh Vietnam

How to Monetize a Blog

Focus heavily on your niche to monetize your blog effectively. I'd suggest only promoting products or services, which relate specifically to your niche of choice. I run a blog about sharing moneymaking tips to help you live the Internet lifestyle. Knowing this, I should only monetize around products related to this niche.

Monetizing happens after matriculating. Money flows in through your blog after you've studied successful online money makers, taken notes on their strategies, put the strategies into practice, and persisted like heck in building your reputation and credibility.

The number one factor in monetizing your blog is the quality of your content. **You need to be a content commando.**

Kathmandu Nepal

The number two factor is building your friend network to expand your presence and establish trust. Your content does the selling and your network amplifies your reach. Create astounding content and make friends to effectively monetize your blog.

How long does it take to start making money online?

Typically it takes 6 months to a year to start making money online if you follow a proven system based on creating and targeting content and making connections. I did not make money online regularly for some 3 years after starting my journey.

In retrospect, I can clearly see the mistakes I made. For example, I did some solid content creating but ignored the networking aspect of prospering online. I also opened only one income channel during my first few years online. Both mistakes retarded my online growth.

Create. Connect. I struggled for years but the delay in prospering was not necessary. Learn from my lesson. Dive in from day one using a proven system of publishing content and making friends in your niche to cut down your learning curve and accelerate your income streams.

Bonus C

Originally, I was going to close this book with the 5th C (Cash), but I couldn't do this in good conscience without including an article by Jenny Halasz, one of my main mentors.

Jenny's a true SEO veteran who's been giving solid advice to brands since 2000 and, unlike many other consultants, her sober, common sense instructions have stood the test of time, through Penguin, Panda, Hummingbird, and every other change that's come down the pike.

Bonus

Conclusion

Stop, Start, Continue

The funny thing about SEO is that the more things change, the more they stay the same. The tactics shift, and the penalties increase, and the black hats get smarter, but SEO is still fundamentally just marketing. It's always been the case with traditional marketing (print, TV, radio) that instead of just marketing to the customer, you're also marketing to the channel.

What I mean by this is that ultimately your product or service should be appealing to a target customer, whether it's B2B or B2C. But you have to consider the channel you're promoting it in. In print, you had to squeeze your message into a single 8 ½ by 11 page, or on TV into a 30 second spot. In SEO, it's a certain number of characters, or a certain format. The search engines have rules for websites the way that magazines have rules for font sizes and typefaces.

But here's the thing. I'm from the south, and we have a saying here. You can put lipstick on a pig, and it might make it prettier, but it's still a pig. If you have a website that fundamentally sucks in terms of layout or structure, or a product that doesn't deliver to a need, or a service that talks big, but fails when it comes to keeping people happy, it's just a pig. And you need to examine what underlying issue has to change.

The biggest difference between SEO 15 years ago and SEO today is that the search engines (especially Google) are better at spotting pigs.

If I had to give advice on three things to stop, start, and continue with SEO, it would be these:

STOP trying to game the system. Studying Google's algorithms, patents, and updates is fun if you're into data. But if you're doing it just to reverse-engineer the algorithm, you're going to fail. Google now makes something like 500+ algorithm changes a year. And most of those go unnoticed by everyone except people who were trying to game it.

STOP spraying links all over the web. If you're treating your link building efforts like 'skunk spray' – stinking up the entire area in the hope you'll overtake predators – then you are absolutely doing it wrong. Think about the way you party now compared to the way you partied in college. Moderation! Directory listings are good – in moderation. Guest posts are good – in moderation. Articles are good – in moderation. Do any one of those too much and you'll be the guy passed out in the corner while the party goes on around you. Think about what will help your business, and do that instead.

STOP treating the Internet like a get-rich-quick scheme. The Internet has matured. People expect companies to have great features, great service, and great product selection. It's unlikely that you're going to be the next Facebook or Apple without a tremendous investment in time, technology, and capital.

CONTINUE embracing the power of reviews. 70% of people rely on reviews to make purchasing decisions, according to Google. Companies only get good reviews when they surprise and delight their customers. The old adage is true – make someone happy, they'll tell two friends. Piss them off, they'll tell twenty. Except on the Internet, the ratios are more like 200 to 2,000.

CONTINUE being amazing. At the end of the day, make sure you're building, making, creating, and selling something great. Make people happy or help them solve their problems. Make their lives just a little bit easier. Make sure your site is not just readable on mobile, but mobile friendly. Go the extra mile to provide a pleasant experience with your email campaigns, your coupon experiences, and your customer service. There is nothing better for SEO than a bunch of happy customers.

START thinking about the future. Think about wearables like Google Glass and the iWatch. Realize that the Fitbit, the Garmin, and myriad other tools will become more advanced. Consider critically how your product or service fits in. How will you leverage this new technology in your business?

START developing your entity relationships. Everything is related to something. If your name is Sam, then Sam 'has' car, Sam 'has' house. House 'has' Sam's wife, wife 'has' children. Children 'have' computers, computers 'have' apps. Start thinking in this way to understand why and how schema works. Whether we have to keep tagging everything ourselves or search engines just get more advanced at discovering the relationships themselves, entities are the future of how we'll search.

START bending to the search engines' whim. If they tell you to nofollow, do it. If they give you a new schema tag to use, use it. If they tell you to stand on your head, ask them for how long. Like it or not, the search engines rule SEO. We are free to ignore their recommendations, to block their robots, or ignore their penalties. But it's like the kid at the playground that you don't play nicely with. He will just take his ball and go home. Google doesn't need you. So feel free to question, criticize, or even get irritated by what Google requires. 'But do it anyway.'

START focusing on real metrics. Rankings are nice to track, and they can tell you a lot about things when you view them in categories. Visits are cool, but there's a lot of noise from affiliates, pay to click programs, and DOS attacks. But what really matters at the end of the day is money. So make sure your analytics is set up to track actual goals. Assign a monetary value to them or don't, but make sure you know what contributes to real, actual customers instead of just a first place ranking for your CEO's name.

I think the biggest mistake new SEOs make is taking things at face value. Dr. Pete wrote this amazing open letter to SEOs (moz.com/blog/an-open-letter-to-new-seos), where he hits this right on the head.

Question. Test. Test Again. Build. Destroy.

Just because someone you respect says your Title tag should be 56 characters for maximum click-through doesn't mean it's going to be that way with your business, your industry, your clients. A caveat though. Unless your purpose is purely academic, be careful of falling into the trap of testing all the time and never creating. You have a responsibility to your clients and to yourself to deliver results, not just the results of tests.

Now It's Your Turn

Congratulations! You've made it to the end.

I am grateful that you took the time to read my book. If you acted on even a couple of tips you learned from reading it, I have no doubt your online visibility will increase dramatically.

So, please act on it and keep me posted on your progress on Twitter, using the hashtag #SEOLike5 and tagging my handle (@SearchDecoder) in your updates or questions.

Want more? Get on my mailing list to get awesome free inbound marketing, SEO, and growth hacking tips:

SearchDecoder.com/Newsletter

Good luck!

Made in the USA
Charleston, SC
11 November 2014